THE ULTIMATE PRICING CHEAT SHEET

Unlock the Psychology and Strategies to Dominate Your Market and Maximize Profits

John Goldstein Jr.

THE ULTIMATE PRICING CHEAT SHEET

Copyright © 2024 by John Goldstein Jr.

All rights reserved. No part of this book may be reproduced, stored in a retrieval system, or transmitted in any form or by any means, electronic, mechanical, photocopying, recording, or otherwise, without prior written permission from the publisher, except for brief quotations embodied in critical reviews and certain other noncommercial uses permitted by copyright law.

TABLE OF CONTENTS

Introduction 7

Chapter 1: Understanding Pricing Fundamentals 10

Chapter 2: The Psychology of Pricing 18

Chapter 3: Value-Based Pricing 26

Chapter 4: Cost-Based Pricing 35

Chapter 5: Competitive Pricing Strategies 44

Chapter 6: Dynamic Pricing 53

Chapter 7: Price Discrimination Techniques 62

Chapter 8: Price Elasticity of Demand 73

Chapter 9: Navigating Price Wars 82

Chapter 10: Premium Pricing Strategies 92

Chapter 11: Skimming Pricing Tactics 102

Chapter 12: Penetration Pricing Strategies 112

Chapter 13: Promotional Pricing Techniques 121

Chapter 14: Discount Pricing Strategies 131

Chapter 15: Understanding Price Sensitivity 140

Chapter 16: Price Positioning in the Market 148

Chapter 17: Price Negotiation Skills 157

Chapter 18: Communicating Pricing Effectively 164

Chapter 19: Pricing Analytics for Decision Making 171

Chapter 20: Pricing Optimization Techniques 180

Chapter 21: Leading Your Team in Pricing Strategy Development 189

Chapter 22: Future Trends in Pricing Strategies 198

Introduction

What if I told you that a single decision could transform your business, elevate your profits, and crush your competition? Pricing isn't just a number—it's your secret weapon. In today's hyper-competitive world, the companies that master pricing don't just survive—they thrive. They lead. They dominate.

The truth is, pricing is far more than slapping a price tag on a product or service. It's about understanding your market, your customers, and the hidden psychological triggers that drive purchasing decisions. Pricing is where strategy meets psychology, where data meets intuition, and where business owners and executives can gain the ultimate edge.

Think about it: every pricing decision you make tells your customers who you are. Are you the premium choice that screams quality, or the affordable option that wins by volume? Are you positioning yourself as innovative and exclusive, or accessible and disruptive? The way you price shapes your brand, builds your relationships with customers, and ultimately defines your destiny in the marketplace.

But let's be real—pricing is complex. It's one of the most challenging, and often misunderstood, elements of business strategy. That's exactly why this book exists. I'm here to guide you, step by step, through the strategies, tactics, and tools you need to not just compete but to win. Whether you're launching a groundbreaking product, navigating a brutal price war, or fine-tuning your pricing for maximum profit, this book is your roadmap.

By the time you finish reading, you'll understand how to:

- Leverage value-based pricing to tap into your customers' desires and maximize profitability.
- Navigate the delicate balance of price sensitivity and demand elasticity to grow sales without compromising your margins.
- Master dynamic and competitive pricing strategies that respond to market shifts in real time.
- Avoid the pitfalls of discounting and promotions while driving real value and loyalty.
- Use advanced pricing analytics to make decisions with confidence and precision.

This is your moment to master the art and science of

pricing. It's not just a business strategy—it's a competitive superpower. Together, we'll uncover the tools, frameworks, and psychological insights that will make you unstoppable in your market.

So, let's begin this journey. It's time to take control of your pricing, unlock your business's full potential, and secure your place at the top. Let's make it happen.

Chapter 1: Understanding Pricing Fundamentals

Defining Pricing and Its Role in Business

Pricing is more than just a number slapped on a product or service; it is a critical aspect of business strategy that can determine the success or failure of an organization. It is the mechanism through which a company communicates value to its customers and, ultimately, influences their purchasing decisions. Understanding pricing fundamentals is essential for any business leader, as it directly affects revenue, profitability, and market positioning.

At its core, pricing can be defined as the process of determining what a company will receive in exchange for its products or services. This seemingly simple definition belies the complexity and strategic importance of pricing. Pricing is influenced by a variety of factors, including production costs, market demand, competition, and the perceived value of the product or service. It is a dynamic process that requires constant evaluation and adjustment in response to market conditions and consumer behavior.

The role of pricing in business extends beyond mere revenue generation. It serves as a tool for market segmentation, brand positioning, and competitive advantage. For instance, a luxury brand may employ premium pricing to convey exclusivity and superior quality, while a budget brand may adopt a low-cost pricing strategy to attract price-sensitive consumers. The chosen pricing strategy can significantly influence a company's market perception and customer loyalty.

Moreover, pricing is a crucial element of the marketing mix, often referred to as the "four Ps"—Product, Price, Place, and Promotion. While product quality and promotional efforts are essential, the price ultimately determines whether a consumer will make a purchase. Therefore, effective pricing strategies are integral to achieving overall business objectives and sustaining competitive success.

Key Concepts in Pricing Models and Strategies

To navigate the complexities of pricing, it is essential to

understand the various models and strategies that can be employed. Pricing models provide a framework for setting prices based on different factors, while pricing strategies outline the approach a company will take to achieve its pricing objectives. Here, we will explore some key concepts in pricing models and strategies.

1. Cost-Based Pricing: This model involves setting prices based on the costs of production plus a markup for profit. It is straightforward and ensures that costs are covered, but it may not always align with market demand or consumer willingness to pay.

2. Value-Based Pricing: Contrary to cost-based pricing, value-based pricing focuses on the perceived value of a product or service to the customer. This approach requires a deep understanding of customer needs and preferences, allowing businesses to charge a premium for products that deliver exceptional value.

3. Competitive Pricing: This strategy involves setting prices based on competitors' pricing structures. Companies may choose to price their products similarly, lower, or higher than competitors, depending on their market positioning and value proposition.

4. Dynamic Pricing: Dynamic pricing is a flexible pricing strategy that adjusts prices in real-time based on market

demand, competitor pricing, and other factors. This approach is commonly used in industries such as travel and hospitality, where prices fluctuate based on availability and demand.

5. Penetration Pricing: This strategy involves setting a low initial price to attract customers and gain market share quickly. While it can be effective for entering new markets, businesses must carefully consider the long-term implications of maintaining low prices.

6. Skimming Pricing: Skimming pricing involves setting a high initial price for a new product and gradually lowering it over time. This approach is often used for innovative products with little competition, allowing companies to maximize profits from early adopters.

7. Psychological Pricing: This strategy leverages psychological factors to influence consumer behavior. For example, pricing a product at $9.99 instead of $10.00 can create the perception of a better deal, even if the difference is minimal.

8. Promotional Pricing: This involves temporarily reducing prices to stimulate sales or attract customers. Promotional pricing can take various forms, including discounts, coupons, and limited-time offers.

9. **Price Discrimination:** Price discrimination is the practice of charging different prices to different customers for the same product or service. This strategy can maximize revenue but must be implemented carefully to avoid alienating customers.

10. **Price Elasticity of Demand:** Understanding price elasticity is crucial for pricing decisions. Price elasticity measures how sensitive consumer demand is to changes in price. Products with high elasticity will see significant changes in demand with small price adjustments, while inelastic products remain stable despite price changes.

11. **Price Positioning:** This concept involves determining how a product's price relates to its competitors and the overall market. Effective price positioning helps businesses communicate their value proposition and differentiate themselves from competitors.

12. **Price Negotiation:** Negotiation skills are essential for businesses that engage in direct sales or B2B transactions. Effective price negotiation can lead to mutually beneficial agreements while maintaining profitability.

These key concepts provide a foundation for understanding the intricacies of pricing in business. As we delve deeper into this book, we will explore each of these concepts in greater detail, offering insights and practical strategies for mastering pricing models, tactics, and optimization.

The Importance of Pricing Strategy in Business

A well-defined pricing strategy is crucial for achieving business success. It not only impacts revenue and profitability but also shapes customer perceptions and brand loyalty. Here are several reasons why pricing strategy is vital for businesses:

1. Revenue Generation: Pricing is one of the most direct ways to influence revenue. A well-structured pricing strategy can maximize sales and profit margins, contributing significantly to the bottom line.

2. Market Positioning: Pricing communicates a brand's market positioning. A premium price can signal high quality and exclusivity, while a low price can attract budget-conscious consumers. The chosen pricing strategy should align with the overall brand identity and target market.

3. Competitive Advantage: In a competitive marketplace, pricing can be a differentiating factor. Companies that understand their competitors' pricing strategies can position themselves effectively to capture market share.

4. Customer Perception: Pricing influences how customers perceive a product or service. A high price may suggest superior quality, while a low price may raise concerns about quality. Businesses must carefully consider how their pricing aligns with customer expectations.

5. Profitability: Effective pricing strategies can enhance profitability by optimizing price points and minimizing price sensitivity. Understanding the relationship between price and demand allows businesses to make informed pricing decisions that maximize profit margins.

6. Flexibility and Adaptability: A dynamic pricing strategy allows businesses to respond quickly to market changes, competitor actions, and consumer behavior. This adaptability is crucial in today's fast-paced business environment.

7. Long-Term Sustainability: A well-thought-out pricing strategy contributes to long-term business sustainability. By balancing profitability with customer satisfaction, businesses can build lasting relationships with their customers.

8. Market Research and Insights: Developing a pricing strategy requires thorough market research and analysis. This process provides valuable insights into customer

behavior, market trends, and competitive landscape, enabling informed decision-making.

Conclusion

In conclusion, understanding pricing fundamentals is essential for any business leader seeking to master pricing strategies, tactics, and optimization for competitive success. Pricing is not merely a financial decision; it is a strategic tool that influences every aspect of a business, from revenue generation to market positioning and customer perception.

As we continue through this book, we will explore various pricing models and strategies in greater detail, equipping you with the knowledge and skills necessary to navigate the complexities of pricing in today's competitive landscape. By mastering pricing fundamentals, you can unlock the secrets to effective pricing models, strategies, and psychology, ultimately driving maximum profitability and market dominance.

Chapter 2: The Psychology of Pricing

In the realm of pricing strategies, understanding the psychological factors that influence consumer behavior is paramount. Pricing is not merely a reflection of cost; it is a complex interplay of perception, value, and emotion. This chapter delves into the psychological underpinnings of pricing, examining how consumer behavior shapes pricing strategies and the profound impact that pricing psychology has on sales performance.

How Consumer Behavior Influences Pricing

Consumer behavior is a multifaceted construct that encompasses the decision-making processes of individuals when they select, purchase, use, and dispose of products and services. It is influenced by a myriad of factors, including cultural, social, personal, and psychological elements. Understanding these influences is crucial for businesses aiming to optimize their pricing strategies.

The Role of Perception in Pricing

Perception plays a critical role in how consumers respond to prices. The price of a product can evoke different meanings and emotions, and consumers often base their purchasing decisions not solely on the numerical value but on what that price signifies. For instance, a higher price can be perceived as an indicator of quality, while a lower price may suggest inferior quality. This phenomenon is known as price perception.

To illustrate, consider the luxury goods market. Brands like Rolex and Louis Vuitton command premium prices, and consumers are often willing to pay these prices because they associate them with exclusivity, status, and superior craftsmanship. Conversely, a discount retailer may thrive on low prices, appealing to cost-conscious consumers who prioritize affordability over prestige.

Anchoring Effect and Pricing

The anchoring effect is a cognitive bias that influences decision-making, where individuals rely heavily on the first piece of information they encounter when making judgments. In pricing, this can manifest in various ways. For example, if a consumer sees a product priced at $100, and then encounters a similar product priced at $70, the latter may seem like a bargain, even if its actual value does not justify the price difference.

Retailers often exploit this phenomenon by strategically placing high-priced items next to lower-priced alternatives, creating a mental anchor that makes the latter appear more appealing. This tactic not only enhances the perceived value of the lower-priced item but also encourages consumers to make quicker purchasing decisions.

The Influence of Pricing Tactics on Consumer Behavior

Pricing tactics can significantly shape consumer behavior. Limited-time offers, discounts, and bundling are just a few examples of how businesses can create a sense of urgency or added value that drives sales. The concept of scarcity, for instance, can trigger a fear of missing out (FOMO), compelling consumers to act swiftly to secure a deal before it vanishes.

Moreover, the psychology of discounts plays a crucial role in consumer decision-making. A 20% discount on a product may resonate more with consumers than a $10 reduction, even if both scenarios result in the same final price. This is due to the way consumers mentally process percentages versus absolute values. Understanding these nuances allows businesses to craft pricing strategies that resonate with their target audience.

The Impact of Pricing Psychology on Sales

The relationship between pricing psychology and sales performance is profound. By leveraging psychological principles, businesses can create pricing strategies that not only attract customers but also enhance their overall buying experience. This section explores the various psychological factors that impact sales and how businesses can harness these insights to optimize their pricing models.

The Power of Price Framing

Price framing refers to the way in which a price is presented to consumers. The context in which a price is communicated can significantly influence how it is perceived. For example, a product priced at $99.99 may seem more appealing than one priced at $100, even though the difference is negligible. This is known as the "left-digit effect," where consumers focus on the first digit of a price rather than the total amount.

Furthermore, framing a price in relation to its value can enhance consumer perception. For instance, a subscription service that highlights the monthly cost as a small fraction of the annual fee can create a perception of value, making it easier for consumers to justify the expense. By strategically framing prices, businesses can enhance the attractiveness of their offerings and encourage sales.

The Role of Social Proof in Pricing

Social proof is a psychological phenomenon where individuals look to the behaviors and opinions of others to guide their own actions. In the context of pricing, social proof can be leveraged to enhance perceived value. For instance, displaying customer reviews, testimonials, or ratings alongside a product's price can create a sense of credibility and trust, making consumers more likely to purchase.

Additionally, utilizing scarcity and urgency can amplify social proof. Limited-time offers or low stock alerts can create a sense of urgency, leading consumers to act quickly for fear of missing out. This tactic not only drives sales but also reinforces the idea that the product is desirable, as evidenced by its limited availability.

The Effect of Pricing on Brand Perception

Pricing is a key determinant of brand perception. Consumers often associate price with quality, and a well-defined pricing strategy can shape how a brand is perceived in the marketplace. Brands that position themselves as premium often adopt higher pricing strategies to reinforce their image, while value-oriented brands focus on affordability.

However, it is essential to strike a balance. Overpricing can alienate potential customers, while underpricing may lead to perceptions of inferiority. Businesses must carefully consider their target audience and brand positioning to develop pricing strategies that align with their overall marketing goals.

Practical Applications of Pricing Psychology

Understanding the psychology of pricing is not just an academic exercise; it has practical implications for businesses seeking to enhance their sales performance. This section outlines actionable strategies that organizations can implement to leverage pricing psychology effectively.

Conducting Consumer Research

The foundation of effective pricing psychology lies in understanding consumer behavior. Businesses should invest in consumer research to gain insights into their target audience's preferences, motivations, and perceptions. Surveys, focus groups, and A/B testing can provide valuable data that informs pricing strategies.

For example, a company launching a new product may

conduct surveys to gauge consumer reactions to different price points. This data can guide pricing decisions, ensuring that the final price aligns with consumer expectations and perceived value.

Testing Pricing Strategies

Pricing is not a set-it-and-forget-it endeavor; it requires continuous testing and optimization. Businesses should experiment with different pricing strategies to determine what resonates best with their audience. This could involve testing various price points, discount structures, or promotional tactics to identify the most effective approach.

A/B testing can be particularly valuable in this regard. By presenting different pricing options to separate groups of consumers, businesses can analyze which approach yields the highest conversion rates and overall sales.

Building a Strong Value Proposition

A compelling value proposition is essential for successful pricing strategies. Businesses should clearly articulate the unique benefits and value that their products or services offer. This not only justifies the price but also enhances consumer perception.

For instance, a software company may emphasize the

time-saving features of its product, illustrating how it can reduce operational costs for businesses. By effectively communicating value, organizations can foster a stronger connection between pricing and consumer benefits.

The psychology of pricing is a powerful tool that can significantly impact consumer behavior and sales performance. By understanding the underlying psychological principles that influence pricing perceptions, businesses can craft strategies that resonate with their target audience. From leveraging the anchoring effect to employing effective price framing, organizations can optimize their pricing models for maximum profitability.

As we move forward in this book, we will explore various pricing strategies and models, building on the foundation laid in this chapter. By mastering the psychology of pricing, businesses can unlock the secrets to effective pricing strategies, ultimately achieving competitive success in the marketplace.

Chapter 3: Value-Based Pricing

In the realm of pricing strategies, one approach stands out for its potential to maximize profitability while simultaneously aligning with customer expectations: value-based pricing. This chapter delves into the principles of value-based pricing, exploring how businesses can implement these strategies effectively to achieve maximum profitability and maintain a competitive edge in the marketplace.

Principles of Value-Based Pricing

Value-based pricing is fundamentally about understanding and leveraging the perceived value of a product or service from the customer's perspective. Unlike cost-based pricing, which focuses on the costs incurred in producing a product and then adds a markup for profit, value-based pricing emphasizes the value that a product delivers to its customers. This approach requires a deep understanding of customer needs, preferences, and the competitive landscape.

Understanding Perceived Value

Perceived value is the worth that a product or service holds in the eyes of the customer. It is influenced by various factors, including the quality, brand reputation, customer service, and the unique benefits that the product offers. Businesses that successfully identify and enhance perceived value can command higher prices, as customers are often willing to pay a premium for products that they believe offer superior benefits.

To effectively implement a value-based pricing strategy, businesses must first conduct thorough market research to understand their target customers. This involves gathering insights about customer preferences, pain points, and the specific benefits they seek from a product. Surveys, focus groups, and customer interviews can be instrumental in uncovering these insights.

Differentiation and Value Proposition

A key aspect of value-based pricing is differentiation. In a crowded marketplace, products that stand out due to unique features or benefits can justify a higher price point. Crafting a compelling value proposition is essential for communicating the unique value that a product offers. This proposition should clearly articulate why a customer should choose one product over another, highlighting the specific benefits that address their needs.

For instance, consider a company that produces high-end kitchen appliances. By emphasizing the durability, energy efficiency, and innovative technology of their products, they can position themselves as a premium brand. This differentiation allows them to implement a value-based pricing strategy that reflects the superior value their products deliver.

Implementing Value-Based Strategies for Maximum Profitability

Implementing a successful value-based pricing strategy requires careful planning and execution. Here are several key steps that businesses can follow to ensure they maximize profitability through value-based pricing:

1. Conduct Thorough Market Research

As previously mentioned, understanding customer perceptions of value is crucial. Businesses should invest time and resources into conducting comprehensive market research. This includes analyzing competitors, understanding market trends, and gathering feedback directly from customers.

Utilizing tools like customer segmentation can help

businesses identify different groups within their target market, allowing for tailored value propositions that resonate with specific customer segments. For example, a software company might find that small businesses prioritize affordability, while larger enterprises value advanced features and support.

2. Develop a Clear Value Proposition

Once businesses have a solid understanding of their customers, the next step is to develop a clear and compelling value proposition. This proposition should concisely convey the unique benefits of the product, addressing customer pain points and highlighting how the product meets their needs better than alternatives.

A well-crafted value proposition not only helps in pricing decisions but also serves as a foundation for marketing and sales strategies. It should be communicated consistently across all customer touchpoints, from advertising to sales presentations.

3. Align Pricing with Value Perception

With a clear value proposition in place, businesses must align their pricing with the perceived value of their offerings. This involves setting prices that reflect the benefits provided to customers while remaining competitive within the market.

One effective technique is to use tiered pricing models, where different pricing levels correspond to varying levels of service or product features. This approach allows customers to choose the option that best fits their needs and budget, while also providing opportunities for upselling.

4. Communicate Value Effectively

Effective communication of value is essential for successful implementation of a value-based pricing strategy. Businesses should ensure that their marketing materials, sales pitches, and customer interactions consistently highlight the benefits and unique features of their products.

Storytelling can be a powerful tool in this regard. By sharing customer success stories or testimonials, businesses can illustrate the real-world impact of their products, reinforcing the perceived value in the minds of potential customers.

5. Monitor and Adjust Pricing Strategies

Value-based pricing is not a one-time exercise; it requires ongoing monitoring and adjustment. Market conditions, customer preferences, and competitor actions can all impact perceived value, necessitating regular reassessment of pricing strategies.

Businesses should establish key performance indicators (KPIs) to track the effectiveness of their pricing strategies. Metrics such as sales volume, profit margins, and customer satisfaction can provide valuable insights into whether the current pricing aligns with customer perceptions of value.

Case Study: Value-Based Pricing in Action

To illustrate the effectiveness of value-based pricing, let's examine a case study of a software company that successfully implemented this strategy.

Background

XYZ Software, a company specializing in project management tools, faced stiff competition from both established players and new entrants in the market. Their product offered unique features, such as real-time collaboration and advanced analytics, but they struggled with pricing their software effectively.

Steps Taken

1. Market Research: XYZ Software conducted extensive market research to understand customer needs and preferences. They discovered that many customers valued collaboration features highly, particularly in remote work environments.

2. Value Proposition Development: Based on their findings, XYZ Software crafted a value proposition that emphasized the benefits of real-time collaboration and productivity enhancements. They positioned their software as a tool that not only improved project outcomes but also fostered team engagement.

3. Tiered Pricing Model: The company introduced a tiered pricing model, offering three different packages: Basic, Professional, and Enterprise. Each package provided varying levels of features, with the Professional and Enterprise packages priced to reflect the enhanced value they offered.

4. Effective Communication: XYZ Software revamped its marketing materials to highlight customer success stories that showcased the benefits of their software. They used testimonials from satisfied customers to reinforce the value proposition.

5. Monitoring and Adjusting: After implementing the new pricing strategy, XYZ Software closely monitored sales performance and customer feedback. They found that the Professional package was particularly popular, leading them to consider additional features that could be added to the Enterprise package to further enhance its value.

Results

As a result of their value-based pricing strategy, XYZ Software experienced a significant increase in sales and customer satisfaction. By aligning their pricing with perceived value, they were able to command higher prices while simultaneously attracting more customers who recognized the benefits of their product.

Challenges in Value-Based Pricing

While value-based pricing presents numerous advantages, it is not without its challenges. Businesses may encounter several obstacles when implementing this strategy, including:

1. Difficulty in Assessing Perceived Value

Determining perceived value can be complex, as it varies from customer to customer. What one customer views as a significant benefit may not resonate with another. Businesses must invest time in understanding these differences and tailoring their value propositions accordingly.

2. Risk of Underpricing or Overpricing

Misjudging customer perceptions can lead to underpricing or overpricing products. Underpricing can erode profit margins, while overpricing may deter potential customers. Continuous market research and feedback collection are essential to mitigate these risks.

3. Competition and Market Dynamics

In a competitive market, other players may respond to value-based pricing strategies with their own adjustments. Businesses must remain vigilant and responsive to changes in the competitive landscape to maintain their pricing advantage.

Value-based pricing is a powerful strategy that allows businesses to maximize profitability by aligning prices with customer perceptions of value. By conducting thorough market research, developing clear value propositions, and effectively communicating value, companies can implement successful value-based pricing strategies that not only enhance profitability but also foster long-term customer loyalty.

As the marketplace continues to evolve, businesses that embrace value-based pricing will be better positioned to thrive in a competitive environment. By understanding the principles of value-based pricing and applying them effectively, organizations can unlock new opportunities for growth and success in their pricing strategies.

Chapter 4: Cost-Based Pricing

In the intricate world of pricing strategies, cost-based pricing stands as a fundamental approach that emphasizes the importance of understanding internal cost structures. This chapter delves into the nuances of cost-based pricing, exploring its advantages, disadvantages, and the critical role it plays in shaping pricing strategies for businesses across various industries.

Understanding Cost Structures and Their Impact on Pricing

At its core, cost-based pricing revolves around the costs incurred in the production of goods and services. This involves a thorough analysis of both fixed and variable costs. Fixed costs remain constant regardless of the volume of goods produced, such as rent, salaries, and equipment depreciation. Variable costs, on the other hand, fluctuate with production levels, including raw materials, labor, and utilities.

Understanding these cost structures is crucial for businesses aiming to set prices that not only cover expenses but also ensure profitability. A comprehensive cost analysis enables businesses to determine the minimum price at which they can sell their products while still maintaining a healthy profit margin.

Fixed Costs: These are expenses that do not change with the level of goods or services produced. For example, if a company pays $10,000 monthly for its office lease, this cost remains the same regardless of how many units it produces.

Variable Costs: These costs vary directly with the level of production. For example, if a manufacturer produces 1,000 units of a product, the cost of raw materials will increase proportionally with the number of units produced.

Total Cost: The total cost of production is the sum of fixed and variable costs. Understanding this total cost is essential for determining the minimum selling price.

To illustrate, consider a company that manufactures custom furniture. The fixed costs may include the lease of the workshop and salaries of permanent staff, while variable costs may consist of wood, fabric, and labor associated with each piece of furniture produced. By calculating the total cost of production for each item, the company can establish a baseline price that ensures all costs are covered.

Advantages of Cost-Based Pricing

Cost-based pricing offers several advantages that can make it an appealing strategy for businesses:

1. Simplicity: One of the most significant advantages of cost-based pricing is its straightforward nature. Businesses can easily calculate the total cost of production and add a markup to determine the selling price. This simplicity makes it accessible for small businesses and startups that may not have extensive pricing expertise.

2. Cost Recovery: By ensuring that prices cover all costs, businesses can maintain financial stability. This is particularly important for companies with high fixed costs, as they need to sell a certain volume of products to break even.

3. Predictable Profit Margins: Cost-based pricing allows businesses to set consistent profit margins. Once the cost structure is established, companies can apply a standard markup to their prices, leading to predictable profit levels.

4. Reduced Price Competition: In markets where many competitors use cost-based pricing, businesses can avoid price wars by maintaining a focus on their cost structures. This approach helps companies establish a sustainable pricing model that is less influenced by competitor pricing.

5. Ease of Implementation: Cost-based pricing can be easily implemented across various products and services, making it a versatile strategy for businesses with diverse offerings.

Disadvantages of Cost-Based Pricing

While cost-based pricing has its advantages, it is not without its drawbacks. Businesses must be cautious of the following disadvantages:

1. Ignores Market Demand: One of the most significant criticisms of cost-based pricing is that it does not take into account consumer demand or market trends. A business may set prices based solely on costs, but if consumers are unwilling to pay that price, sales may suffer.

2. Potential for Overpricing: If a company miscalculates its costs or applies an excessive markup, it risks pricing itself out of the market. This is particularly true in highly competitive industries where consumers have numerous alternatives.

3. Lack of Flexibility: Cost-based pricing can lead to rigidity in pricing strategies. Businesses may find it challenging to adjust prices in response to changing market conditions or consumer preferences, which can hinder their competitiveness.

4. Inadequate Profit Maximization: By focusing primarily on costs, businesses may miss opportunities to maximize profits through value-based pricing strategies. This approach limits their ability to capture consumer surplus, which is the difference between what consumers are willing to pay and what they actually pay.

5. Encourages Inefficiency: Cost-based pricing can inadvertently encourage inefficiency within organizations. If employees know that all costs will be covered regardless of performance, there may be less incentive to minimize expenses or improve productivity.

Implementing Cost-Based Pricing Strategies

To effectively implement cost-based pricing strategies, businesses must follow several essential steps:

1. Conduct a Thorough Cost Analysis: The first step in implementing cost-based pricing is to conduct a comprehensive analysis of all costs associated with production. This includes both fixed and variable costs, as well as any indirect costs that may impact pricing.

2. Determine Desired Profit Margin: Once businesses have a clear understanding of their cost structures, they should establish a desired profit margin. This margin will guide the markup applied to the total cost to arrive at the final selling price.

3. Set the Selling Price: With the total cost and desired profit margin in mind, businesses can calculate the selling price. This is done by adding the desired profit margin to the total cost.

{Selling Price} = {Total Cost} + {Desired Profit Margin}

4. Monitor and Adjust: After implementing cost-based pricing, businesses should continuously monitor their costs and market conditions. If costs change or if consumer demand shifts, adjustments to the pricing strategy may be necessary to maintain profitability.

5. Evaluate Competitor Pricing: While cost-based pricing focuses on internal costs, it is essential to remain aware of competitor pricing strategies. Businesses should regularly assess how their prices compare to those of competitors and make adjustments as needed.

6. Communicate Value: Even with a cost-based pricing strategy, businesses must effectively communicate the value of their products or services to consumers. This can help justify the pricing and enhance consumer

perception.

Case Study: A Practical Example of Cost-Based Pricing

To better understand the application of cost-based pricing, let's consider a hypothetical case study of a small bakery, "Sweet Delights."

Background: Sweet Delights specializes in artisanal bread and pastries. The owner, Sarah, wants to establish a pricing strategy that ensures all costs are covered while also generating a profit.

Cost Analysis: Sarah conducts a thorough analysis of her costs. She identifies the following:

- Fixed Costs:

  - Rent: $1,500/month

  - Salaries: $2,000/month

  - Utilities: $300/month

  - Equipment depreciation: $200/month

- Variable Costs (per loaf of bread):

  - Flour: $0.50

  - Yeast: $0.05

  - Water: negligible

- Labor: $0.75

- Packaging: $0.20

Total variable cost per loaf: $1.50

Total Costs: Sarah calculates her fixed costs per loaf based on her production volume. If she produces 1,000 loaves a month, her fixed costs per loaf would be:

Total cost per loaf = (Fixed costs / number of loafs: $4,000 / 1,000 = $4) + Variable costs per loaf = $4.00 + $1.50 = $5.50.

Desired Profit Margin: Sarah decides she wants a profit margin of 40%. To calculate her selling price:

{Selling Price} = {Total Cost} + ({Total Cost} * {Desired Profit Margin}) = 5.50 + (5.50 * 0.40) = 5.50 + 2.20 = 7.70

Thus, Sarah sets the selling price of each loaf of bread at $7.70.

Monitoring and Adjusting: After a few months, Sarah reviews her costs and finds that the price of flour has increased due to supply chain issues. She decides to adjust her selling price accordingly. By recalculating her costs and desired profit margin, she determines that the new selling price for her bread should be $8.20.

Conclusion: Through diligent cost analysis and strategic

pricing, Sweet Delights successfully implements a cost-based pricing strategy that ensures all costs are covered while allowing for a healthy profit margin. This approach not only stabilizes the bakery's finances but also provides a framework for future pricing decisions.

Cost-based pricing is a foundational strategy that provides businesses with a clear understanding of their cost structures and the necessary framework for setting prices. While it offers advantages such as simplicity and cost recovery, it also presents challenges related to market demand and flexibility. By implementing effective cost analysis, establishing desired profit margins, and continuously monitoring costs and market conditions, businesses can leverage cost-based pricing to achieve sustainable profitability.

In the following chapters, we will explore alternative pricing strategies, including competitive pricing and value-based pricing, which can complement or enhance the cost-based approach. By understanding the full spectrum of pricing strategies, businesses can position themselves for long-term success in an ever-evolving marketplace.

Chapter 5: Competitive Pricing Strategies

In the ever-evolving landscape of business, pricing stands as a pivotal element that can define an organization's market position and profitability. Competitive pricing strategies are not merely about setting a price lower than your competitors; they encompass a complex interplay of market analysis, consumer perception, and business objectives. This chapter delves into the intricacies of competitive pricing, providing a comprehensive framework for developing a pricing strategy that not only considers competitors but also aligns with your brand's value proposition and market goals.

Analyzing Competitors' Pricing Models

At the heart of competitive pricing strategies lies a thorough analysis of competitors' pricing models. Understanding how competitors set their prices can provide valuable insights into market dynamics and consumer expectations. This analysis can be broken down into several key components:

Identifying Competitors

The first step in analyzing competitors' pricing models is to identify who your competitors are. This may include direct competitors—those offering similar products or services—and indirect competitors—those providing alternatives that fulfill the same customer need. Mapping out the competitive landscape allows businesses to position themselves effectively.

Gathering Pricing Data

Once you have identified your competitors, the next step is to gather pricing data. This can be achieved through various methods, including:

1. Market Research: Conducting surveys and focus groups to understand consumer perceptions of competitors' pricing.

2. Mystery Shopping: Engaging in competitive intelligence by purchasing from competitors to gauge their pricing strategy firsthand.

3. Online Tools: Utilizing pricing comparison websites and platforms to track competitors' prices in real-time.

Analyzing Pricing Strategies

After gathering data, it is essential to analyze the pricing strategies employed by competitors. This involves looking at:

- Price Levels: Are competitors pricing their products higher, lower, or at parity with the market average?

- Discounting Practices: Do competitors frequently offer discounts or promotions, and how do these affect their perceived value?

- Bundling and Packaging: Are there unique bundling strategies that competitors use to enhance perceived value?

By understanding these elements, businesses can identify gaps in the market and opportunities for differentiation.

Understanding Market Positioning

Competitors' pricing strategies are often a reflection of their overall market positioning. For instance, a luxury brand may adopt a premium pricing strategy to reinforce its high-end image, whereas a budget brand may focus on cost leadership to attract price-sensitive customers. Analyzing how competitors position themselves helps businesses determine where they fit within the market and how they can effectively compete.

Developing a Competitive Pricing Strategy

With a solid understanding of competitors' pricing models, the next step is to develop a competitive pricing strategy. This involves several strategic considerations:

Setting Pricing Objectives

Before establishing a pricing strategy, it is crucial to define clear pricing objectives. These objectives may include:

- Maximizing Profitability: Setting prices that optimize profit margins.

- Increasing Market Share: Pricing products to attract a larger customer base.

- Enhancing Brand Image: Establishing a price point that reflects the brand's value proposition.

By aligning pricing objectives with broader business goals, companies can create a coherent pricing strategy that supports overall success.

Choosing a Pricing Strategy

There are various pricing strategies that businesses can adopt, each with its own advantages and disadvantages. Some common approaches include:

1. Penetration Pricing: Setting a low initial price to gain market share quickly. This strategy can be effective in crowded markets but may lead to lower profit margins in the short term.

2. Price Skimming: Introducing a product at a high price and gradually lowering it over time. This approach can maximize profits from early adopters but may alienate price-sensitive customers.

3. Competitive Pricing: Setting prices based on competitors' pricing. This strategy can help maintain market position but may lead to price wars if not managed carefully.

4. Value-Based Pricing: Pricing products based on the perceived value to the customer rather than the cost of production. This strategy can enhance profitability but requires a deep understanding of consumer perceptions.

Implementing Price Adjustments

Once a pricing strategy is chosen, it is crucial to implement price adjustments thoughtfully. This may involve:

- Monitoring Competitors: Continuously tracking competitors' pricing changes to remain competitive.

- Customer Feedback: Gathering insights from customers

regarding their price sensitivity and perceived value.

- Market Trends: Staying informed about market trends and economic factors that may impact pricing.

Communicating Pricing Changes

Effective communication is vital when implementing pricing changes. Customers should be informed of any adjustments, especially if they result in price increases. Transparency in pricing can help maintain customer trust and loyalty. Strategies for communicating pricing changes include:

- Clear Messaging: Clearly articulate the reasons for price changes, such as increased costs or enhanced product features.

- Customer Engagement: Engage with customers through social media and email newsletters to explain pricing decisions and gather feedback.

Case Studies in Competitive Pricing

To illustrate the effectiveness of competitive pricing strategies, let's examine a few case studies from various industries.

Case Study 1: Airline Industry

In the airline industry, competitive pricing strategies are

crucial for market survival. Airlines often engage in dynamic pricing, adjusting fares based on demand, competition, and other factors. For instance, during peak travel seasons, airlines may raise prices significantly, while offering discounts during off-peak times to attract price-sensitive travelers. By analyzing competitors' pricing and adjusting their strategies accordingly, airlines can maximize revenue while remaining competitive.

Case Study 2: Retail Sector

In the retail sector, companies like Walmart have successfully implemented competitive pricing strategies by leveraging their economies of scale. Walmart's "Everyday Low Prices" strategy positions the brand as a cost leader, attracting price-sensitive customers while maintaining profitability through high sales volumes. The company continuously monitors competitors' prices and adjusts its pricing strategies to ensure it remains the lowest-cost provider in the market.

Case Study 3: Technology Industry

In the technology industry, companies like Apple often employ value-based pricing strategies. While their products are priced higher than competitors, the brand's perceived value allows them to maintain strong profit margins. Apple's pricing strategy is supported by extensive market research, customer feedback, and a deep understanding of consumer behavior. By effectively communicating the unique value of their products, Apple successfully justifies its premium pricing.

Challenges in Competitive Pricing Strategies

While competitive pricing strategies can be highly effective, they also come with challenges. Some of these challenges include:

Price Wars

Engaging in price wars with competitors can erode profit margins and damage brand perception. Businesses must be cautious when adjusting prices to avoid triggering a race to the bottom. Strategies to mitigate this risk include:

- Focusing on Value: Emphasizing the unique value proposition of products rather than solely competing on price.

- Differentiation: Developing unique features or services that set the brand apart from competitors.

Consumer Perception

Consumer perception plays a significant role in

competitive pricing strategies. If customers perceive a price as too low, they may question the quality of the product. Conversely, if a price is perceived as too high, it may deter potential buyers. Balancing price with perceived value is essential for maintaining brand integrity.

Market Fluctuations

Economic factors, such as inflation or changes in consumer spending habits, can impact pricing strategies. Businesses must remain agile and adaptable, continuously monitoring market conditions and adjusting pricing strategies accordingly.

Competitive pricing strategies are integral to achieving market success and profitability. By thoroughly analyzing competitors' pricing models and developing a thoughtful pricing strategy, businesses can position themselves effectively in the market. However, it is essential to remain vigilant, adapting to market dynamics and consumer perceptions to maintain a competitive edge. In the following chapters, we will explore additional pricing strategies and tactics that can further enhance your pricing approach and drive business success.

Chapter 6: Dynamic Pricing

Dynamic pricing is a sophisticated pricing strategy that adjusts prices in real-time based on market demand, consumer behavior, and other external factors. This chapter delves into the mechanics of dynamic pricing models, explores their applications across various industries, and examines case studies that highlight successful implementations of dynamic pricing strategies.

Understanding Dynamic Pricing

Dynamic pricing, often referred to as surge pricing or demand pricing, is a flexible pricing strategy where prices are adjusted based on current market demands rather than fixed pricing models. The fundamental principle behind dynamic pricing is to optimize revenue by responding to market fluctuations and consumer behavior.

The rise of technology and data analytics has amplified the effectiveness of dynamic pricing. Businesses can now leverage real-time data, including consumer behavior, competitor pricing, inventory levels, and external factors such as weather and events, to determine optimal pricing at any given moment. This approach is prevalent in industries such as e-commerce, travel, hospitality, and entertainment, where demand can vary significantly based on time, season, and other factors.

The Mechanics of Dynamic Pricing Models

Dynamic pricing models can be categorized into several types, each with its unique mechanics and applications:

1. Time-Based Pricing: This model adjusts prices based on the time of day, week, or year. For example, airlines often increase prices for flights during peak travel seasons or weekends while offering discounts during off-peak times.

2. Demand-Based Pricing: Prices are set based on the level of consumer demand. For instance, ride-sharing services like Uber utilize demand-based pricing, adjusting fares based on the number of riders and available drivers in a specific area.

3. Competitor-Based Pricing: This model involves monitoring competitors' prices and adjusting accordingly. Retailers often employ this strategy, especially during sales events or holidays, to remain competitive.

4. Segmented Pricing: Different prices are charged for various customer segments based on their willingness to pay. For example, software companies may offer discounts to students or non-profit organizations.

5. Dynamic Yield Management: This advanced model utilizes algorithms to predict demand and adjust prices in real-time. It is commonly used in industries with perishable goods or limited inventory, such as airlines and hotels.

Implementing Dynamic Pricing Strategies

Implementing dynamic pricing requires a strategic approach to ensure that the pricing changes align with business objectives while providing value to customers. Here are key steps to successfully implement dynamic pricing strategies:

1. Data Collection and Analysis: Gather data from various sources, including sales history, customer behavior, market trends, and competitor pricing. This data will serve as the foundation for your dynamic pricing model.

2. Define Pricing Rules: Establish clear rules for how prices will be adjusted based on different variables. For example, you might decide to increase prices by a certain

percentage when demand exceeds a predefined threshold.

3. Utilize Technology: Invest in pricing software or tools that can analyze data and adjust prices in real-time. These tools can automate the pricing process, allowing for more efficient and accurate pricing adjustments.

4. Monitor and Adjust: Continuously monitor the performance of your dynamic pricing strategy. Analyze sales data, customer feedback, and market conditions to make necessary adjustments to your pricing model.

5. Communicate with Customers: Transparency is essential when implementing dynamic pricing. Clearly communicate the reasons for price changes to customers, emphasizing the value they receive.

Case Studies on Successful Dynamic Pricing

To illustrate the effectiveness of dynamic pricing, let's explore several case studies across different industries.

Case Study 1: Airlines

The airline industry is a pioneer of dynamic pricing, utilizing sophisticated algorithms to adjust ticket prices based on demand, competition, and booking patterns. For instance, airlines often raise prices as the departure date approaches and seats fill up.

A notable example is Delta Airlines, which employs a dynamic pricing model that considers factors such as historical booking data, current market demand, and competitor pricing. By analyzing these variables, Delta can optimize ticket prices, maximizing revenue while ensuring competitive positioning.

Case Study 2: E-Commerce

E-commerce giants like Amazon have mastered dynamic pricing. Their pricing algorithms analyze millions of data points, including competitor prices, customer browsing behavior, and inventory levels, to adjust prices frequently throughout the day.

During peak shopping periods, such as Black Friday or Cyber Monday, Amazon employs dynamic pricing to offer competitive deals while maximizing profit margins. This strategy not only drives sales but also enhances customer loyalty, as consumers perceive Amazon as a platform that offers the best prices.

Case Study 3: Ride-Sharing Services

Uber's dynamic pricing model, commonly known as surge pricing, adjusts fares based on demand and supply in real-time. During peak hours or adverse weather conditions, prices increase to incentivize more drivers to get on the road while managing the high demand from riders.

This approach has been effective in balancing supply and demand, ensuring that riders can always find a ride while providing drivers with the motivation to work during busy times. Despite facing criticism during price surges, Uber has maintained transparency about its pricing model, helping to mitigate customer dissatisfaction.

Case Study 4: Hospitality

Hotels also utilize dynamic pricing to maximize occupancy rates and revenue. For example, Marriott International employs a dynamic pricing strategy that adjusts room rates based on factors such as seasonality, local events, and booking trends.

By analyzing data on customer behavior and market conditions, Marriott can optimize pricing to attract guests during low-demand periods while capitalizing on high-demand seasons. This approach has resulted in increased occupancy rates and higher overall revenue.

Challenges and Considerations in Dynamic Pricing

While dynamic pricing offers significant advantages, it also presents challenges that businesses must navigate:

1. Customer Perception: Frequent price changes can lead to customer frustration and dissatisfaction. Businesses must communicate clearly about pricing changes and the

rationale behind them to maintain trust.

2. Competitive Landscape: The competitive nature of dynamic pricing means that businesses must constantly monitor competitors' pricing strategies. Failure to do so could result in losing market share.

3. Data Security and Privacy: Collecting and analyzing customer data raises concerns about privacy and data security. Businesses must ensure compliance with regulations and protect customer information.

4. Algorithm Bias: Relying on algorithms for pricing decisions can lead to unintended biases. Businesses must regularly review and adjust their algorithms to ensure fairness and accuracy.

5. Regulatory Compliance: In some industries, dynamic pricing may attract regulatory scrutiny. Businesses must be aware of legal implications and ensure compliance with pricing regulations.

Best Practices for Successful Dynamic Pricing

To maximize the effectiveness of dynamic pricing, businesses should consider the following best practices:

1. Test and Iterate: Implement A/B testing to evaluate different pricing strategies and identify what works best for your target audience.

2. Leverage Customer Feedback: Actively seek customer feedback on pricing changes to gauge their reactions and make necessary adjustments.

3. Integrate with Marketing: Align dynamic pricing strategies with marketing campaigns to create a cohesive approach that enhances customer engagement.

4. Educate Your Team: Ensure that your team understands the dynamics of dynamic pricing and is equipped to communicate effectively with customers.

5. Stay Agile: The market is constantly evolving, and businesses must remain agile in their pricing strategies. Regularly review and adjust your dynamic pricing model based on market trends and consumer behavior.

Conclusion

Dynamic pricing represents a powerful tool for businesses seeking to optimize revenue and respond to market fluctuations. By understanding the mechanics of dynamic pricing models, implementing effective strategies, and learning from successful case studies, organizations can harness the potential of dynamic pricing to achieve competitive success.

As the landscape of pricing continues to evolve, businesses must remain vigilant in their approach to dynamic pricing, ensuring they adapt to changing market conditions while maintaining a focus on customer satisfaction. By doing so, they can unlock the full potential of dynamic pricing and position themselves for long-term success in an increasingly competitive marketplace.

Chapter 7: Price Discrimination Techniques

Price discrimination, a strategy that involves charging different prices to different customers for the same product or service, is a powerful tool in the arsenal of pricing strategies. This chapter delves into the nuances of price discrimination techniques, their applications across various industries, and the ethical and legal considerations that accompany them. By understanding the mechanics of price discrimination, businesses can optimize their pricing strategies to maximize profitability while maintaining customer satisfaction.

Understanding Price Discrimination and Its Applications

Price discrimination can be categorized into three main types: first-degree, second-degree, and third-degree price discrimination. Each type utilizes different criteria for setting prices and targets distinct customer segments.

First-Degree Price Discrimination

First-degree price discrimination, also known as personalized pricing, involves charging each customer the maximum price they are willing to pay. This strategy requires a deep understanding of individual customer preferences and behaviors. Businesses that successfully implement first-degree price discrimination can capture the entire consumer surplus—the difference between what consumers are willing to pay and what they actually pay.

For example, in the realm of online retail, companies like Amazon utilize advanced algorithms to analyze customer data and adjust prices in real-time based on purchasing behavior, browsing history, and even geographic location. This approach allows them to tailor prices to individual customers, maximizing revenue from each sale.

Second-Degree Price Discrimination

Second-degree price discrimination occurs when prices vary based on the quantity consumed or the product version purchased, rather than individual customer characteristics. This method encourages customers to self-select into different pricing tiers based on their preferences and willingness to pay.

A classic example of second-degree price discrimination is the tiered pricing model used by software companies.

For instance, a software provider might offer a basic version of its product at a lower price, while charging a premium for a full-featured version. Customers who value additional features are incentivized to upgrade, while those with more limited needs can opt for the basic version, allowing the company to maximize revenue from different customer segments.

Third-Degree Price Discrimination

Third-degree price discrimination involves segmenting customers into distinct groups based on observable characteristics, such as age, location, or purchasing behavior, and charging different prices to each group. This strategy is commonly seen in industries such as travel and entertainment, where discounts are offered to students, seniors, or members of specific organizations.

For instance, airlines often implement third-degree price discrimination by offering discounted fares to students or seniors. Similarly, movie theaters may provide reduced ticket prices for children and seniors, allowing them to attract a broader customer base while optimizing revenue.

Ethical Considerations and Legal Implications

While price discrimination can be an effective pricing strategy, it is not without its ethical and legal challenges.

Businesses must navigate the fine line between maximizing profitability and ensuring fair treatment of customers. Understanding the ethical implications of price discrimination is essential for maintaining brand integrity and customer trust.

Ethical Considerations

The ethical considerations surrounding price discrimination primarily revolve around fairness and transparency. Customers may perceive price discrimination as unfair if they feel they are being charged more than others for the same product or service. This perception can lead to dissatisfaction and damage to the brand's reputation.

To mitigate these concerns, businesses should ensure that their pricing strategies are transparent and justifiable. Providing clear explanations for pricing differences, such as the rationale behind discounts for specific groups, can help foster customer understanding and acceptance.

Moreover, businesses should avoid discriminatory practices that exploit vulnerable populations. For example, charging significantly higher prices for essential goods in low-income areas can lead to public backlash and legal repercussions.

Legal Implications

From a legal standpoint, price discrimination is governed by various laws and regulations that vary by jurisdiction. In the United States, the Robinson-Patman Act prohibits certain forms of price discrimination that can harm competition. This legislation aims to ensure that businesses do not engage in unfair pricing practices that disadvantage competitors.

To comply with legal standards, businesses must carefully assess their pricing strategies to ensure they do not inadvertently violate anti-discrimination laws. Consulting legal experts and conducting regular audits of pricing practices can help organizations navigate the complex landscape of pricing regulations.

Implementing Price Discrimination Strategies

Successfully implementing price discrimination strategies requires a thorough understanding of customer segments, effective communication, and robust data analytics. Here are key steps to consider when developing and executing price discrimination techniques:

1. Identify Customer Segments

The first step in implementing price discrimination is to identify distinct customer segments based on observable characteristics. Conducting market research and analyzing customer data can help businesses uncover valuable insights into customer preferences, behaviors, and willingness to pay.

Segmentation can be based on various factors, including demographics, purchasing history, and geographic location. By understanding the unique needs and preferences of each segment, businesses can tailor their pricing strategies accordingly.

2. Develop Pricing Models

Once customer segments are identified, businesses can develop pricing models that align with the preferences and behaviors of each group. This may involve creating tiered pricing structures, offering discounts for specific demographics, or implementing personalized pricing strategies.

For example, a hotel chain may develop a pricing model that offers discounted rates for seniors and families, while charging higher rates for business travelers during peak seasons. By aligning pricing with customer segments, businesses can optimize revenue while enhancing customer satisfaction.

3. Leverage Data Analytics

Data analytics plays a crucial role in the successful implementation of price discrimination strategies. By leveraging advanced analytics tools, businesses can gather insights into customer behavior, preferences, and price sensitivity.

Utilizing predictive analytics can help organizations forecast demand and optimize pricing in real-time. For instance, e-commerce platforms can analyze customer browsing and purchasing patterns to adjust prices dynamically, ensuring they capture maximum revenue from each transaction.

4. Communicate Clearly

Effective communication is essential for the successful implementation of price discrimination strategies. Businesses should strive to provide clear explanations for pricing differences to avoid confusion and dissatisfaction among customers.

Transparency in pricing can foster trust and loyalty among customers. For example, if a company offers discounts for students, clearly communicating the eligibility criteria and the rationale behind the discount can enhance customer acceptance.

5. Monitor and Adjust

Finally, businesses should continuously monitor the effectiveness of their price discrimination strategies and be prepared to make adjustments as needed. Regularly analyzing sales data, customer feedback, and market trends can provide valuable insights into the performance of pricing strategies.

If certain pricing models are not yielding the desired results, businesses should be willing to experiment with different approaches. Flexibility and adaptability are key to successfully navigating the dynamic landscape of pricing.

Case Studies in Price Discrimination

To illustrate the effectiveness of price discrimination techniques, let's examine a few case studies from various industries that have successfully implemented these strategies.

Case Study 1: Airlines and Dynamic Pricing

Airlines are well-known for their use of price discrimination strategies, particularly dynamic pricing. By analyzing factors such as demand, booking time, and customer segmentation, airlines can adjust ticket prices in real-time.

For instance, during peak travel seasons, airlines may

charge significantly higher prices for tickets purchased closer to the departure date. Conversely, early bird discounts encourage travelers to book in advance, allowing airlines to maximize revenue from different customer segments.

This dynamic pricing strategy has proven effective in optimizing revenue while accommodating diverse customer needs. By offering a range of pricing options, airlines can attract both budget-conscious travelers and those willing to pay a premium for last-minute bookings.

Case Study 2: Software Companies and Tiered Pricing

Many software companies utilize tiered pricing models to implement second-degree price discrimination. For example, a popular project management software provider offers multiple subscription tiers based on features and user capacity.

The basic plan, designed for small teams, is priced affordably, while the premium plan, which includes advanced features and support, is priced higher. This approach allows the company to cater to a wide range of customers, from startups to large enterprises, maximizing revenue from each segment.

By clearly communicating the value of each tier and providing incentives for upgrades, the software provider effectively captures customer willingness to pay while fostering loyalty among users.

Case Study 3: Retail and Student Discounts

Retailers often implement third-degree price discrimination by offering discounts to specific demographics, such as students. A well-known clothing retailer provides a 10% discount to students with valid identification.

This strategy not only attracts price-sensitive students but also fosters brand loyalty among a younger demographic. By communicating the discount clearly and promoting it through social media channels, the retailer enhances its appeal to this customer segment while optimizing revenue.

Price discrimination techniques offer businesses a powerful means of optimizing pricing strategies and maximizing profitability. By understanding the different types of price discrimination and their applications, organizations can tailor their pricing approaches to meet the unique needs of diverse customer segments.

However, businesses must navigate the ethical and legal considerations that accompany price discrimination. By maintaining transparency, ensuring fairness, and complying with relevant regulations, organizations can implement effective pricing strategies while preserving customer trust.

As the competitive landscape continues to evolve, mastering price discrimination techniques will be essential for businesses seeking to achieve market dominance and drive sustainable growth. By leveraging data analytics, communicating effectively, and continuously monitoring pricing strategies, organizations can unlock the full potential of price discrimination and secure a competitive edge in their respective industries.

Chapter 8: Price Elasticity of Demand

Introduction to Price Elasticity of Demand

Price elasticity of demand (PED) is a critical concept in pricing strategy that measures how sensitive the quantity demanded of a good or service is to a change in its price. Understanding PED is essential for businesses aiming to optimize their pricing strategies, maximize profitability, and maintain a competitive edge in the marketplace. This chapter will delve into the intricacies of price elasticity, how to measure it, its significance in pricing decisions, and strategies to optimize pricing based on elasticity insights.

Understanding Price Elasticity

Price elasticity of demand is defined as the percentage change in quantity demanded divided by the percentage change in price. Mathematically, it can be expressed as:

{Price Elasticity of Demand (PED)} = {Change in Quantity Demanded} \ {Change in Price}

The value of PED can be classified into three categories:

1. Elastic Demand (PED > 1): This indicates that consumers are highly responsive to price changes. A small increase in price leads to a significant drop in quantity demanded, and vice versa. Luxury goods often fall into this category.

2. Inelastic Demand (PED < 1): In this case, consumers are less responsive to price changes. A price increase may lead to a small decrease in quantity demanded, making it easier for businesses to raise prices without losing significant sales. Necessities like basic food items and medications typically exhibit inelastic demand.

3. Unitary Elastic Demand (PED = 1): Here, the percentage change in quantity demanded is equal to the percentage change in price. This scenario is relatively rare but can occur in certain market conditions.

The Importance of Price Elasticity in Pricing Strategy

Understanding price elasticity is vital for several reasons:

1. Revenue Management: Knowing whether a product is elastic or inelastic helps businesses make informed decisions about pricing adjustments. For elastic products, lowering prices could lead to increased sales and higher overall revenue, while for inelastic products, raising

prices might enhance revenue without significantly affecting sales volume.

2. Market Positioning: Price elasticity provides insights into consumer behavior and preferences. Businesses can use this information to position their products effectively in the market, ensuring that pricing aligns with consumer expectations and perceived value.

3. Cost Recovery: For businesses with high fixed costs, understanding the elasticity of demand is crucial for recovering costs. If demand is elastic, businesses may need to keep prices lower to maintain sales volumes, while inelastic demand allows for higher pricing strategies.

4. Competitive Analysis: Analyzing the elasticity of competitors' products can inform a company's pricing strategy. Understanding how competitors' pricing affects their sales can lead to better strategic positioning and pricing decisions.

Measuring Price Elasticity of Demand

To measure price elasticity effectively, businesses can utilize various methods, including:

1. Historical Data Analysis: By examining sales data over time, businesses can assess how changes in price have

affected quantity demanded. This method involves statistical analysis and regression modeling to derive the elasticity coefficient.

2. Surveys and Consumer Research: Conducting surveys can provide insights into consumer behavior and their price sensitivity. Businesses can ask consumers how likely they are to purchase a product at various price points, providing qualitative data that can be quantified into elasticity measures.

3. Experimental Pricing: Implementing controlled pricing experiments, such as A/B testing, allows businesses to observe how changes in price affect sales in real-time. This method can yield immediate feedback on price elasticity.

4. Competitor Benchmarking: Analyzing competitors' pricing strategies and their impact on sales can offer insights into the elasticity of similar products in the market. This approach requires careful observation and analysis of market trends.

Factors Influencing Price Elasticity of Demand

Several factors can influence the price elasticity of demand for a product:

1. Availability of Substitutes: The more substitutes

available for a product, the more elastic the demand. If consumers can easily switch to alternatives when prices rise, demand becomes more sensitive to price changes.

2. Necessity vs. Luxury: Necessities tend to have inelastic demand, while luxury goods are often elastic. Consumers will continue purchasing necessities regardless of price changes, while luxury goods may see significant drops in demand with price increases.

3. Proportion of Income: Products that take up a larger portion of a consumer's income tend to have more elastic demand. For example, a significant increase in the price of a car will likely lead to a more substantial reduction in quantity demanded compared to a small increase in the price of a loaf of bread.

4. Time Horizon: Demand elasticity can vary over time. In the short term, consumers may be less responsive to price changes, while in the long term, they may adjust their purchasing behavior based on price changes.

5. Brand Loyalty: Strong brand loyalty can lead to inelastic demand. Consumers who are loyal to a brand may continue purchasing despite price increases, as they perceive added value in the brand.

Strategies to Optimize Pricing Based on Elasticity

Understanding price elasticity allows businesses to develop targeted pricing strategies that align with consumer behavior and market conditions. Here are several strategies to optimize pricing based on elasticity insights:

1. Dynamic Pricing: Implementing dynamic pricing strategies allows businesses to adjust prices in real-time based on demand fluctuations. For example, airlines and hotels often use dynamic pricing models to maximize revenue during peak travel seasons or special events.

2. Promotional Pricing: For products with elastic demand, promotional pricing can stimulate sales. Limited-time discounts or special offers can attract price-sensitive consumers and increase overall sales volume.

3. Tiered Pricing: Offering different pricing tiers based on features or service levels can cater to varying consumer price sensitivities. This strategy allows businesses to capture both price-sensitive customers and those willing to pay a premium for additional value.

4. Bundling Products: Bundling complementary products can enhance perceived value and encourage purchases. If one product is elastic and the other is inelastic, bundling can help maintain overall sales while optimizing pricing.

5. Value Communication: For inelastic products,

emphasizing the product's value can justify higher prices. Effective marketing that highlights unique features, benefits, and brand reputation can reinforce consumer perceptions and support premium pricing.

6. Regular Review and Adjustment: Regularly reviewing pricing strategies based on market conditions, competitor actions, and consumer feedback is essential. Continuous monitoring of price elasticity can inform necessary adjustments to pricing strategies.

Case Studies on Price Elasticity in Action

To illustrate the practical application of price elasticity in pricing strategies, let's examine a few case studies:

Case Study 1: Airline Industry

The airline industry is a prime example of price elasticity in action. Airlines utilize dynamic pricing models that adjust ticket prices based on demand, time of booking, and remaining seat availability. During peak travel seasons, airlines may increase prices significantly due to high demand, while offering discounts during off-peak times to stimulate sales. This strategy maximizes revenue while considering the elastic nature of their ticket prices.

Case Study 2: Consumer Electronics

Consumer electronics companies often face elastic

demand, particularly for new product launches. For instance, when a new smartphone is released, early adopters may be willing to pay a premium. However, as time passes and competitors release similar models, demand becomes more elastic. Companies frequently implement price drops after the initial launch period to stimulate sales and remain competitive in a rapidly evolving market.

Case Study 3: Fast-Moving Consumer Goods (FMCG)

FMCG companies often deal with inelastic demand for essential products, such as food and household items. These companies can increase prices without significantly affecting sales volume. However, they also use promotional pricing strategies, such as discounts or loyalty programs, to attract price-sensitive consumers and maintain market share in competitive categories.

Conclusion

Price elasticity of demand is a vital element of effective pricing strategies. By understanding how consumers respond to price changes, businesses can make informed decisions that enhance profitability and market positioning. Whether through dynamic pricing, promotional strategies, or value communication, leveraging insights from price elasticity can lead to optimized pricing models that align with consumer behavior and market dynamics.

As businesses navigate the complexities of pricing in an ever-evolving marketplace, mastering the concept of price elasticity will be instrumental in achieving competitive success and long-term profitability. By continuously analyzing and adapting pricing strategies based on elasticity insights, companies can position themselves for sustained growth and market dominance.

Chapter 9: Navigating Price Wars

Understanding Price Wars and Their Implications

In the competitive landscape of modern business, price wars can emerge as a significant challenge for organizations striving for market dominance. A price war typically occurs when two or more companies engage in aggressive price reductions to capture market share, often leading to a downward spiral of prices. While the immediate goal may be to outmaneuver competitors and attract price-sensitive customers, the long-term consequences of such strategies can be detrimental to profitability, brand perception, and overall market health.

Price wars can be triggered by various factors, including economic downturns, the entry of new competitors, technological advancements, or shifts in consumer preferences. Understanding the underlying motivations and dynamics of price wars is essential for leaders and teams tasked with navigating these turbulent waters.

Organizations must recognize that engaging in a price war is not merely a tactical decision; it is a strategic maneuver with far-reaching implications.

The implications of price wars extend beyond mere financial performance. They can alter competitive dynamics, reshape consumer perceptions, and even impact the overall industry landscape. Companies that engage in price wars may experience short-term gains in market share, but these gains often come at the expense of long-term profitability. As prices are slashed, profit margins shrink, leading to a potential cycle of cost-cutting measures that can compromise product quality, customer service, and brand integrity.

Moreover, price wars can set a precedent for future pricing behavior within the industry. Once a company lowers its prices, it may find it challenging to raise them again without facing backlash from consumers who have come to expect lower prices. This can lead to a race to the bottom, where competitors continuously undercut each other, resulting in a market characterized by diminished profitability and increased volatility.

Strategies to Survive and Thrive in Price Wars

To effectively navigate price wars, organizations must adopt a multifaceted approach that encompasses strategic foresight, tactical agility, and a deep understanding of their market and customers. Here are several strategies to consider:

1. Reassess Value Proposition

Before engaging in a price war, it is crucial for organizations to reassess their value proposition. What unique benefits do they offer that justify their prices? By emphasizing the value their products or services provide, companies can differentiate themselves from competitors and reduce the likelihood of being dragged into a price war. This may involve enhancing product features, improving customer service, or offering bundled solutions that deliver greater value to customers.

2. Focus on Customer Segmentation

Understanding customer segments is vital in times of price wars. Not all customers are price-sensitive; some may prioritize quality, brand reputation, or unique features over price. By identifying and targeting segments that value these attributes, companies can maintain their pricing strategies without compromising their overall profitability. Tailoring marketing efforts to resonate with these segments can create a loyal customer base that is less likely to be swayed by aggressive pricing tactics.

3. Implement Dynamic Pricing Strategies

Dynamic pricing allows organizations to adjust their prices in real-time based on market conditions, demand fluctuations, and competitor pricing. By leveraging data analytics and technology, companies can optimize pricing strategies to remain competitive without engaging in a full-scale price war. This approach enables businesses to respond swiftly to market changes while maximizing revenue opportunities.

4. Enhance Customer Loyalty Programs

Building strong customer loyalty can serve as a buffer against the impact of price wars. By investing in loyalty programs that reward repeat customers, organizations can create a sense of value that goes beyond price. Customers who feel appreciated and valued are less likely to switch to competitors solely based on price. Additionally, loyal customers can act as brand advocates, helping to attract new customers through positive word-of-mouth.

5. Communicate Transparently

In the midst of a price war, transparent communication with customers is essential. Organizations should clearly articulate the reasons behind pricing decisions and emphasize the value they continue to provide. This transparency can foster trust and loyalty, even in challenging pricing environments. Customers are more likely to remain loyal to brands that communicate openly and maintain their commitment to quality and service.

6. Diversify Product Offerings

Having a diverse product portfolio can help organizations weather the storm of price wars. By offering a range of products at different price points, companies can cater to various customer segments and mitigate the impact of aggressive pricing from competitors. This strategy allows businesses to maintain profitability while still appealing to price-sensitive customers with lower-priced options.

7. Monitor Competitor Behavior

Staying informed about competitor pricing strategies and market trends is critical during price wars. Organizations should invest in competitive intelligence to track pricing changes, promotional activities, and market positioning. By understanding the competitive landscape, companies can make informed decisions about their pricing strategies and respond proactively to shifts in the market.

8. Evaluate Cost Structure

Engaging in a price war often necessitates a thorough evaluation of an organization's cost structure. Identifying areas where costs can be reduced without compromising quality can provide the necessary flexibility to adjust prices competitively. This may involve renegotiating supplier contracts, optimizing operational efficiencies, or streamlining processes to enhance profitability.

9. Engage in Collaborative Pricing

In some cases, collaborating with competitors on pricing strategies can be a viable option. While this may seem counterintuitive, engaging in discussions with industry peers can lead to mutually beneficial agreements that stabilize pricing within the market. Collaborative pricing initiatives can help prevent destructive price wars and foster a healthier competitive environment.

10. Prepare for Post-War Recovery

Once a price war subsides, organizations must be prepared for recovery. This involves reassessing pricing strategies, rebuilding brand perception, and reestablishing customer loyalty. Companies should take proactive steps to communicate the value of their products and services, reinforcing their commitment to quality and customer satisfaction. Recovery may also involve strategic pricing adjustments to return to profitability while maintaining a competitive edge.

Case Studies: Successful Navigation of Price Wars

To illustrate the effectiveness of these strategies, let's explore a few case studies of companies that successfully navigated price wars while maintaining profitability and brand integrity.

Case Study 1: Airline Industry Dynamics

The airline industry is notorious for its price wars, often triggered by new entrants attempting to capture market share. A notable example is the competition between Southwest Airlines and legacy carriers. Southwest Airlines differentiated itself by focusing on customer service, efficiency, and a no-frills approach. While competitors engaged in price slashing, Southwest maintained its pricing strategy by emphasizing its unique value proposition, which resonated with customers seeking a reliable and enjoyable travel experience.

By not succumbing to the pressure of a price war, Southwest Airlines successfully captured a loyal customer base and expanded its market presence. The airline's commitment to quality service and transparent communication fostered customer loyalty, allowing it to thrive even in a challenging pricing environment.

Case Study 2: Retail Giants and Discounting

In the retail sector, companies like Walmart and Target often find themselves in price wars, particularly during seasonal sales. Walmart's strategy of everyday low pricing (EDLP) has allowed it to compete effectively without engaging in aggressive discounting. By focusing on operational efficiencies and cost reduction, Walmart can maintain its pricing structure while delivering value to customers.

Target, on the other hand, has positioned itself as a more upscale retailer while still competing on price. During price wars, Target emphasizes its unique offerings, quality products, and customer experience. By maintaining a strong brand identity and focusing on customer loyalty, Target has successfully navigated price wars without sacrificing profitability.

Case Study 3: Technology Sector Challenges

In the technology sector, companies like Apple and Samsung have faced price wars as they compete for market share in the smartphone industry. Apple, known for its premium pricing strategy, has consistently emphasized the quality, innovation, and ecosystem of its products. While competitors may engage in aggressive discounting, Apple focuses on creating a unique value proposition that resonates with its target audience.

Samsung, on the other hand, offers a diverse range of products at various price points, allowing it to cater to different customer segments. By continuously innovating and enhancing its product offerings, Samsung can compete effectively in price-sensitive markets while maintaining profitability.

Conclusion

Navigating price wars requires a strategic approach that balances competitive pricing with a commitment to value and customer loyalty. Organizations must be vigilant in understanding their market dynamics, customer segments, and the implications of engaging in price wars. By reassessing their value propositions, implementing dynamic pricing strategies, and fostering customer loyalty, companies can not only survive but thrive in challenging pricing environments.

Ultimately, the key to successfully navigating price wars lies in adopting a holistic approach that prioritizes long-term sustainability over short-term gains. By focusing on delivering value, maintaining brand integrity, and fostering strong customer relationships, organizations can emerge from price wars stronger and more resilient, ready to seize new opportunities for growth and market dominance.

Chapter 10: Premium Pricing Strategies

In the realm of pricing strategies, premium pricing stands out as a powerful approach that can significantly enhance a brand's market position and profitability. This chapter delves into the intricacies of premium pricing strategies, exploring their definition, market positioning, and the essential elements required to create a compelling value perception for premium products.

Defining Premium Pricing and Its Market Positioning

Premium pricing, often referred to as prestige pricing, is a strategy where a product is priced higher than similar offerings in the market. This strategy is based on the belief that consumers associate higher prices with higher quality, exclusivity, and status. Premium pricing is not merely about setting a high price; it is about positioning the product in a way that justifies that price to the consumer.

The essence of premium pricing lies in creating a

perception of value that transcends the actual cost of production. This perception can stem from various factors, including brand reputation, unique product features, superior quality, and exceptional customer service. Companies employing premium pricing must ensure that every aspect of their product and brand experience aligns with the elevated price point.

The Psychology Behind Premium Pricing

Understanding the psychology of consumers is crucial in effectively implementing premium pricing strategies. Consumers often perceive higher-priced products as being of better quality. This phenomenon is supported by the "price-quality heuristic," where consumers use price as a proxy for quality. In many cases, a higher price can lead to increased desirability, as consumers may believe that they are purchasing something exclusive or superior.

Moreover, premium pricing can create a sense of prestige and status among consumers. Luxury brands like Rolex and Louis Vuitton thrive on this concept, as owning their products often signals wealth and sophistication. This social signaling is a powerful motivator for consumers, and brands that successfully harness this aspect can command significant price premiums.

Creating Value Perception for Premium Products

To successfully implement a premium pricing strategy, businesses must focus on creating a strong value perception among their target audience. Here are several key components to consider:

1. Quality and Craftsmanship

The perceived quality of a product is fundamental to premium pricing. Consumers expect premium products to exhibit superior craftsmanship, materials, and performance. Brands must invest in high-quality materials and skilled labor to ensure that their products meet or exceed consumer expectations. For instance, luxury automobile manufacturers like BMW and Mercedes-Benz prioritize engineering excellence, which justifies their higher price points.

2. Brand Storytelling

A compelling brand narrative can significantly enhance the perceived value of a product. Storytelling allows brands to connect emotionally with consumers, conveying the heritage, mission, and values that underpin the product. For example, brands like Patagonia leverage their commitment to sustainability and environmental responsibility in their storytelling, appealing to consumers who value these principles. This emotional connection can justify a higher price, as consumers feel they are supporting a brand that aligns with their values.

3. Exclusivity and Scarcity

Creating a sense of exclusivity can enhance the perceived value of a product. Limited edition releases, exclusive collaborations, and restricted availability can drive demand for premium products. When consumers believe that a product is scarce or exclusive, they are often willing to pay a premium to secure it. Brands like Supreme have mastered this strategy, creating a cult following through limited drops and collaborations that generate buzz and urgency.

4. Exceptional Customer Experience

The customer experience plays a pivotal role in reinforcing the value of premium products. From the initial point of contact to post-purchase support, every interaction should reflect the brand's commitment to excellence. Premium brands often invest in personalized service, ensuring that customers feel valued and appreciated. For instance, luxury retailers like Neiman Marcus provide personalized shopping experiences, enhancing the overall perception of value.

5. Effective Marketing and Communication

Clear and effective communication of the product's value

proposition is essential in premium pricing strategies. Marketing efforts should focus on highlighting the unique features, benefits, and emotional appeal of the product. Utilizing high-quality visuals, storytelling, and influencer partnerships can amplify the message and reach the target audience effectively. Brands like Apple excel in this area, showcasing their products through sleek advertising campaigns that emphasize innovation and lifestyle.

Implementing Premium Pricing Strategies

Successfully implementing premium pricing strategies requires careful planning and execution. Here are key steps to consider:

1. Market Research and Segmentation

Before adopting a premium pricing strategy, businesses must conduct thorough market research to identify their target audience. Understanding consumer demographics, preferences, and purchasing behaviors is crucial. Segmentation allows brands to tailor their messaging and product offerings to resonate with specific consumer groups who are willing to pay a premium for perceived value.

2. Competitive Analysis

Analyzing the competitive landscape is essential to

determine the feasibility of a premium pricing strategy. Brands should assess their competitors' pricing models, product offerings, and market positioning. Understanding the strengths and weaknesses of competitors can help identify opportunities to differentiate the brand and justify a premium price.

3. Product Development and Innovation

Innovation plays a critical role in maintaining the allure of premium products. Brands should continually invest in product development to enhance features, improve quality, and introduce new offerings. Staying ahead of market trends and consumer demands is essential for sustaining premium pricing. For example, luxury skincare brands often invest in research and development to create cutting-edge products that command higher prices.

4. Monitoring and Adjusting Pricing

Once a premium pricing strategy is in place, businesses must regularly monitor its effectiveness. Analyzing sales data, customer feedback, and market trends can provide valuable insights into the strategy's performance. If sales decline or consumer perception shifts, brands may need to make adjustments to their pricing, product offerings, or marketing strategies to maintain their premium positioning.

Case Studies in Premium Pricing

To illustrate the effectiveness of premium pricing strategies, let's examine a few case studies of successful brands that have mastered this approach.

Case Study 1: Tesla

Tesla has revolutionized the automotive industry with its premium pricing strategy. By positioning itself as a leader in electric vehicle technology, Tesla has successfully commanded higher prices compared to traditional automakers. The brand's focus on innovation, sustainability, and cutting-edge technology has created a strong value perception among consumers. Tesla's marketing emphasizes the environmental benefits and performance of its vehicles, appealing to eco-conscious consumers willing to pay a premium for a sustainable alternative.

Case Study 2: Rolex

Rolex is synonymous with luxury and prestige, and its pricing strategy reflects this image. The brand has maintained its premium positioning through a combination of exceptional craftsmanship, exclusivity, and a rich heritage. Rolex watches are often seen as status symbols, and the brand's limited production runs and high-quality materials justify the steep price tags. Rolex's marketing emphasizes its legacy of precision and excellence, reinforcing the perception of value among consumers.

Case Study 3: Apple

Apple's premium pricing strategy has been integral to its brand identity. The company consistently prices its products higher than competitors, positioning them as high-quality, innovative solutions. Apple's marketing focuses on the seamless integration of hardware and software, user experience, and design aesthetics. The brand's loyal customer base is willing to pay a premium for the Apple experience, which is reinforced by exceptional customer service and a robust ecosystem of products.

Challenges of Premium Pricing Strategies

While premium pricing can yield significant benefits, it is not without challenges. Businesses must navigate several potential pitfalls:

1. Price Sensitivity

Not all consumers are willing to pay a premium for products, and price sensitivity can vary across market segments. Brands must carefully assess their target audience to ensure that the premium pricing strategy aligns with consumer willingness to pay. Conducting surveys and focus groups can help gauge price sensitivity and inform pricing decisions.

2. Market Saturation

In highly competitive markets, premium pricing strategies may face challenges from competitors offering similar products at lower prices. Brands must differentiate themselves through unique value propositions and exceptional customer experiences to maintain their premium positioning.

3. Economic Factors

Economic downturns can impact consumer spending habits, leading to increased price sensitivity. During challenging economic times, consumers may prioritize value over prestige, making it essential for brands to remain agile and responsive to changing market conditions.

Premium pricing strategies can be a powerful tool for brands seeking to enhance their market position and profitability. By creating a strong value perception through quality, storytelling, exclusivity, and exceptional customer experiences, businesses can justify higher prices and cultivate brand loyalty. However, successful implementation requires careful planning, market research, and ongoing monitoring to navigate the challenges that may arise.

As the marketplace continues to evolve, brands that effectively leverage premium pricing strategies while staying attuned to consumer preferences and market dynamics will be well-positioned for success. In the following chapters, we will explore additional pricing tactics, such as skimming and penetration pricing, that can complement premium pricing strategies and further enhance overall business performance.

Chapter 11: Skimming Pricing Tactics

In the competitive landscape of modern business, pricing strategies play a crucial role in determining the success of new products. Among these strategies, skimming pricing stands out as a powerful tool for maximizing revenue and establishing a strong market presence. This chapter delves into the intricacies of skimming pricing tactics, exploring how to implement them effectively and analyze market responses to such strategies.

Understanding Skimming Pricing

Skimming pricing is a strategy that involves setting a high initial price for a new product or service, with the intention of gradually lowering the price over time. This approach is particularly effective for innovative products that have little to no competition at launch. The primary objective of skimming pricing is to "skim" the maximum revenue from segments of the market that are willing to pay a premium for the new offering.

This strategy is often employed in industries characterized by high development costs, such as technology, pharmaceuticals, and luxury goods. By targeting early adopters and consumers who value exclusivity, businesses can recoup their investments quickly before facing competition that typically drives prices down.

The Rationale Behind Skimming Pricing

The rationale for adopting a skimming pricing strategy can be broken down into several key factors:

1. Recouping Development Costs: New products often require significant investment in research and development. A high initial price allows companies to recover these costs rapidly.

2. Targeting Different Market Segments: Skimming pricing enables businesses to segment the market based on price sensitivity. Early adopters, who are less price-sensitive, are likely to purchase at a premium, while more price-sensitive customers can be targeted later as prices decrease.

3. Establishing Brand Prestige: A high price can create a perception of quality and exclusivity. This is particularly important for luxury brands that rely on their image to attract customers.

4. Mitigating Competition: By setting a high price initially, companies can establish a strong market presence and brand loyalty before competitors enter the market.

5. Maximizing Profit Margins: Skimming pricing allows businesses to maximize profit margins during the early stages of a product's lifecycle, providing a financial cushion that can be used for future investments.

Implementing Skimming Pricing Strategies

Successfully implementing a skimming pricing strategy requires careful planning and execution. Here are the steps businesses should consider:

1. Market Research and Analysis

Before launching a product with a skimming pricing strategy, thorough market research is essential. Understanding the target audience, their willingness to pay, and the competitive landscape will help in setting an appropriate initial price. Surveys, focus groups, and competitor analysis can provide valuable insights.

2. Setting the Initial Price

The initial price should reflect the perceived value of the product and the target market segment. It should be high enough to attract early adopters but not so high that it deters potential customers. Consideration of production costs, competitor pricing, and market demand is crucial in this step.

3. Developing a Pricing Timeline

A well-defined pricing timeline is essential for a successful skimming strategy. Businesses should plan when and how to lower prices over time. This could involve setting specific milestones or triggers based on sales performance or market conditions.

4. Communicating Value

Effective communication of the product's value proposition is vital. Marketing efforts should focus on highlighting the unique features and benefits that justify the high price. This can include targeted advertising, public relations campaigns, and influencer partnerships to create buzz and excitement around the product.

5. Monitoring Market Response

Once the product is launched, businesses must closely monitor market response. Sales data, customer feedback, and competitor actions should be analyzed to determine if adjustments to the pricing strategy are necessary. If sales are slower than anticipated, it may be necessary to lower the price sooner than planned.

6. Adjusting the Pricing Strategy

As the market evolves and competition increases, businesses must be prepared to adjust their pricing strategy. This may involve gradually lowering prices to attract more price-sensitive customers or offering promotions to stimulate demand.

Analyzing Market Response to Skimming Strategies

The effectiveness of skimming pricing tactics can be measured through various metrics and indicators. Understanding these metrics will help businesses refine their pricing strategies and improve overall profitability.

1. Sales Volume and Revenue

The primary indicators of a successful skimming pricing strategy are sales volume and revenue. High initial sales figures indicate strong demand among early adopters, while revenue generated during the skimming phase should exceed production and marketing costs.

2. Customer Feedback and Satisfaction

Customer feedback is crucial in assessing the perceived value of the product. Surveys and reviews can provide insights into whether customers believe the product is worth the price. High levels of customer satisfaction can lead to positive word-of-mouth and repeat purchases.

3. Market Share

Monitoring changes in market share can help businesses understand how well their skimming pricing strategy is performing compared to competitors. A growing market share indicates that the product is resonating with consumers and that the pricing strategy is effective.

4. Competitor Reactions

Competitor reactions to a skimming pricing strategy can provide valuable insights. If competitors respond with price cuts or new product launches, it may indicate that the initial pricing was too high or that the market is becoming more competitive.

5. Price Elasticity of Demand

Understanding the price elasticity of demand for the product is essential for evaluating the success of a skimming strategy. If demand is inelastic, it suggests that consumers are willing to pay the higher price. Conversely, if demand is elastic, businesses may need to reconsider their pricing approach.

Case Studies: Successful Skimming Pricing Examples

To illustrate the effectiveness of skimming pricing tactics, let's explore a few case studies of companies that successfully implemented this strategy.

Case Study 1: Apple Inc.

Apple is renowned for its skimming pricing strategy, particularly with the launch of new iPhones. When a new model is released, it is priced at a premium, targeting early adopters who are eager to have the latest technology. As the product matures and newer models are introduced, Apple gradually lowers the price of previous models, making them more accessible to a broader audience. This strategy allows Apple to maximize profits while maintaining brand prestige.

Case Study 2: Sony PlayStation

When Sony launched the PlayStation 4, it set a high initial price to capitalize on the excitement surrounding the console's release. The company targeted hardcore gamers who were willing to pay a premium for cutting-edge technology and exclusive games. Over time, as competition in the gaming market intensified, Sony lowered the price of the PlayStation 4, attracting a larger customer base while continuing to generate revenue from accessories and game sales.

Case Study 3: Pharmaceuticals

The pharmaceutical industry often employs skimming pricing for new drugs. For example, when a groundbreaking medication is introduced, it is priced at a premium to recover research and development costs. As patents expire and generic alternatives enter the market, the price of the original drug is gradually reduced. This approach allows pharmaceutical companies to maximize profits while ensuring that the medication remains accessible to patients over time.

Challenges of Skimming Pricing

While skimming pricing can be a highly effective strategy, it is not without its challenges. Businesses must navigate several potential pitfalls to ensure success:

1. Market Saturation

In highly competitive markets, rapid saturation can occur, leading to increased price competition. If competitors quickly introduce similar products, the effectiveness of a skimming strategy may diminish. Businesses must be prepared to adapt their pricing approach in response to market dynamics.

2. Consumer Perception

If consumers perceive the initial price as unjustifiably high, it may lead to negative brand perception. Companies must effectively communicate the value of their product to justify the premium price and avoid alienating potential customers.

3. Timing of Price Reductions

Determining the optimal timing for price reductions can be challenging. If prices are lowered too quickly, businesses may miss out on potential revenue. Conversely, delaying price reductions may result in lost sales opportunities as competitors gain traction.

4. Regulatory Challenges

In some industries, regulatory bodies may scrutinize pricing strategies, particularly in healthcare and utilities. Companies must ensure that their skimming pricing tactics comply with relevant regulations to avoid legal repercussions.

Conclusion

Skimming pricing tactics can be a powerful tool for businesses looking to maximize revenue from new products. By setting a high initial price and gradually lowering it over time, companies can target different market segments, recoup development costs, and establish brand prestige. However, successful implementation requires careful planning, market research, and a keen understanding of consumer behavior.

As businesses navigate the complexities of skimming

pricing, they must remain vigilant in monitoring market responses and adapting their strategies accordingly. By doing so, they can unlock the full potential of skimming pricing and achieve competitive success in their respective industries.

Chapter 12: Penetration Pricing Strategies

In a competitive marketplace, businesses continuously seek strategies that enable them to capture market share quickly and effectively. Among these strategies, penetration pricing stands out as a powerful tool, particularly for new entrants aiming to establish a foothold in their respective industries. This chapter delves into the nuances of penetration pricing strategies, exploring their benefits, long-term implications, and the critical factors that businesses must consider when implementing such approaches.

Understanding Penetration Pricing

Penetration pricing is a strategy characterized by setting a low initial price for a product or service to attract customers and gain market share quickly. The fundamental idea is to entice consumers who may be hesitant to try a new offering due to price sensitivity or brand loyalty to existing competitors. By lowering the entry barrier through pricing, businesses can stimulate demand, build a customer base, and establish brand recognition in a crowded market.

Benefits of Penetration Pricing for Market Entry

1. Rapid Market Share Acquisition

One of the most significant advantages of penetration pricing is its ability to facilitate rapid market penetration. By offering products or services at a lower price point than competitors, businesses can attract a larger customer base quickly. This influx of customers can help establish a brand presence, leading to increased sales volume and revenue generation.

2. Consumer Trial and Adoption

Penetration pricing encourages consumers to try a new product or service they might have otherwise overlooked. When faced with a lower price, consumers are more likely to experiment with a new offering, which can lead to repeat purchases and brand loyalty if the product meets or exceeds their expectations.

3. Deterrence of Competitors

A low pricing strategy can act as a deterrent to potential competitors. When new entrants observe a market saturated with low-priced offerings, they may be discouraged from entering due to the perceived difficulty of competing against established players. This can create a barrier to entry, allowing the penetrating company to solidify its market position.

4. Economies of Scale

As sales volume increases due to penetration pricing, businesses can benefit from economies of scale. Higher production volumes often lead to lower per-unit costs, which can enhance profitability over time, even if initial margins are thin due to lower pricing.

5. Cross-Selling Opportunities

A larger customer base acquired through penetration pricing can facilitate cross-selling opportunities. Once customers are engaged with one product, businesses can introduce complementary products or services, further driving revenue and enhancing customer lifetime value.

Long-term Implications of Penetration Pricing

While penetration pricing offers numerous short-term benefits, businesses must also consider the long-term implications of this strategy. Below are some critical factors to evaluate:

1. Sustainability of Low Prices

Maintaining low prices over an extended period can be challenging. Businesses must ensure that their cost structures allow for sustainable pricing without compromising quality or service. If costs rise, companies may find it difficult to raise prices without alienating their customer base.

2. Brand Perception

Penetration pricing can impact brand perception. While low prices may attract initial customers, they may also lead consumers to perceive the brand as low-quality or discount-oriented. Businesses must balance penetration pricing with efforts to build a strong brand image that resonates with their target audience.

3. Transitioning to Profitability

As market share is gained, businesses must develop a clear strategy for transitioning from penetration pricing to a more sustainable pricing model. This may involve gradually increasing prices or introducing premium product lines to enhance profitability while retaining customer loyalty.

4. Competitor Response

The competitive landscape can shift rapidly in response to penetration pricing. Competitors may lower their prices or enhance their offerings to retain market share, leading to potential price wars. Businesses must be prepared to adapt their strategies and respond to competitive actions effectively.

5. Customer Expectations

Once customers become accustomed to low prices, they may resist price increases or perceive higher prices as unjustified. Companies must communicate effectively with their customer base to manage expectations and ensure a smooth transition to new pricing structures.

Implementing Penetration Pricing Strategies

To successfully implement penetration pricing strategies, businesses should consider the following steps:

1. Market Research and Analysis

Conduct thorough market research to understand customer needs, preferences, and price sensitivity. Analyzing competitors' pricing strategies and market positioning will also provide insights into potential pricing thresholds and opportunities for differentiation.

2. Clear Value Proposition

Develop a clear value proposition that communicates the benefits of the product or service. This messaging should resonate with target customers and justify the initial low price. Highlighting unique features, quality, or customer service can enhance perceived value.

3. Targeted Marketing Campaigns

Launch targeted marketing campaigns to promote the new offering and its low price. Utilize digital marketing, social media, and other channels to reach potential customers effectively. Emphasize the trial aspect and the limited-time nature of the low pricing to create urgency.

4. Monitoring and Feedback

Continuously monitor customer feedback and sales performance. Understanding customer perceptions and experiences will help businesses make informed decisions about pricing adjustments and product improvements.

5. Strategic Pricing Adjustments

As market share is gained and customer loyalty is established, businesses should develop a plan for gradually adjusting prices. This may involve phased increases or introducing premium versions of the product to cater to different customer segments.

Case Studies in Penetration Pricing

To illustrate the effectiveness of penetration pricing strategies, let's explore a few case studies of successful implementations.

Case Study 1: Netflix

When Netflix first entered the streaming market, it adopted a penetration pricing strategy by offering a low monthly subscription fee compared to traditional cable services. This pricing model attracted a large number of subscribers quickly, allowing Netflix to build a significant customer base. The company invested heavily in original content, enhancing its value proposition and leading to increased customer loyalty. Over time, Netflix gradually raised its subscription prices while maintaining a strong brand image and customer satisfaction.

Case Study 2: Amazon Prime

Amazon Prime is another example of successful penetration pricing. Initially launched with a low annual fee, Amazon Prime attracted millions of subscribers by offering free shipping and access to exclusive content. As the service gained popularity, Amazon expanded its offerings, including streaming services, music, and cloud storage. The initial low pricing created a loyal customer base, and Amazon has since introduced tiered pricing and additional benefits, allowing for increased revenue while maintaining customer satisfaction.

Case Study 3: Xiaomi

Xiaomi, a Chinese electronics company, employed penetration pricing effectively in the smartphone market. By offering high-quality smartphones at significantly lower prices than competitors, Xiaomi quickly gained market share. The company focused on online sales and direct-to-consumer strategies, reducing costs associated with traditional retail. As brand recognition grew, Xiaomi expanded its product range and introduced premium models, allowing for price adjustments while retaining a loyal customer base.

Penetration pricing strategies offer businesses a valuable approach to entering competitive markets and rapidly acquiring market share. By understanding the benefits and long-term implications of this strategy, companies can make informed decisions that align with their overall business objectives. Successful implementation requires careful planning, market analysis, and a commitment to delivering value to customers.

As businesses navigate the complexities of pricing strategies, the lessons learned from case studies and real-world applications can serve as a guide. By balancing short-term gains with long-term sustainability, organizations can leverage penetration pricing to achieve competitive success and drive profitability in an ever-evolving marketplace.

Chapter 13: Promotional Pricing Techniques

Promotional pricing is a powerful tool in the arsenal of pricing strategies that businesses can utilize to stimulate sales, attract new customers, and enhance market share. This chapter delves into the intricacies of designing effective promotional pricing campaigns and measuring their impact on both short-term sales and long-term brand perception.

Understanding Promotional Pricing

Promotional pricing refers to the temporary reduction of prices to increase demand for a product or service. It is often employed during specific periods, such as holidays, product launches, or clearance sales, and can take various forms, including discounts, special offers, and bundling strategies. While the primary objective of promotional pricing is to drive sales volume, it also serves to create urgency among consumers, encouraging them to make purchasing decisions more quickly.

Promotional pricing can be particularly effective in competitive markets where consumers are price-sensitive and have numerous alternatives to choose from. By leveraging promotional pricing, businesses can differentiate themselves, attract attention, and engage potential customers who might otherwise overlook their offerings.

Designing Effective Promotional Pricing Campaigns

To develop a successful promotional pricing campaign, it is essential to follow a structured approach. Here are several key steps to consider:

1. Define Clear Objectives

Before launching a promotional pricing campaign, it is crucial to establish clear objectives. Common goals include:

- Increasing sales volume

- Attracting new customers

- Clearing out inventory

- Raising brand awareness

- Encouraging repeat purchases

Having well-defined objectives will guide the planning process and help measure the campaign's success.

2. Understand Your Target Audience

To design an effective promotional pricing strategy, businesses must have a deep understanding of their target audience. Conducting market research to identify customer preferences, behaviors, and price sensitivity is essential. This information will help tailor promotional offers that resonate with the audience and motivate them to take action.

3. Choose the Right Promotional Pricing Tactics

There are several promotional pricing tactics that businesses can employ, each with its own advantages and potential drawbacks. Some popular tactics include:

- Discounts: Offering temporary price reductions on specific products or services. This can include percentage discounts, fixed-amount discounts, or "buy one, get one free" offers. Discounts are straightforward and can be highly effective in driving immediate sales.

- Bundling: Combining multiple products or services into a single package at a reduced price. Bundling can increase the perceived value of the offer and encourage customers to purchase more items than they initially planned.

- Limited-Time Offers: Creating a sense of urgency by offering discounts or promotions for a limited time. This tactic can motivate consumers to make quick purchasing decisions to avoid missing out on the offer.

- Loyalty Programs: Providing discounts or rewards to repeat customers as a way to encourage brand loyalty. Loyalty programs can help businesses retain customers and increase their lifetime value.

- Seasonal Promotions: Aligning promotional pricing with seasonal events or holidays. This can include back-to-school sales, holiday discounts, or summer clearance events. Seasonal promotions can capitalize on consumer buying patterns and increase sales during peak shopping times.

4. Communicate the Promotion Effectively

Once the promotional pricing strategy is defined, effective communication is key to its success. Businesses should utilize various channels to promote the offer, including:

- Email Marketing: Sending targeted emails to customers and prospects to inform them of the promotion. This can be an effective way to reach existing customers who are already familiar with the brand.

- Social Media: Leveraging social media platforms to create buzz around the promotion. Engaging visuals and compelling messaging can capture the attention of potential customers.

- In-Store Signage: For brick-and-mortar businesses, clear signage can help inform customers of promotional offers as they shop. Well-placed signs can enhance visibility and drive impulse purchases.

- Paid Advertising: Utilizing online and offline advertising to reach a broader audience. This can include pay-per-click ads, print advertisements, or radio spots that highlight the promotional offer.

5. Monitor and Adjust

Once the promotional pricing campaign is launched, it is essential to monitor its performance closely. Key performance indicators (KPIs) to track include:

- Sales volume during the promotional period

- Customer acquisition rates

- Customer retention rates

- Overall profit margins

By analyzing these metrics, businesses can assess the effectiveness of the promotional pricing strategy and make necessary adjustments in real time. If certain tactics are underperforming, adjustments can be made to optimize the campaign for better results.

Measuring the Impact of Promotional Pricing

Measuring the impact of promotional pricing is critical for understanding its effectiveness and informing future pricing strategies. Businesses can employ various methods to evaluate the success of their promotional campaigns:

1. Sales Analysis

One of the most straightforward methods of measuring the impact of promotional pricing is through sales analysis. By comparing sales figures during the promotional period to previous periods, businesses can assess the effectiveness of the promotion. Key metrics to consider include:

- Sales Growth: Analyzing the percentage increase in sales during the promotional period compared to a baseline period.

- Sales Volume: Evaluating the total number of units sold during the promotion to determine if the pricing strategy successfully drove higher sales.

- Customer Traffic: Monitoring foot traffic or website

visits during the promotional period can provide insights into how well the promotion attracted customers.

2. Customer Feedback

Collecting customer feedback during and after the promotional pricing campaign can provide valuable insights into its effectiveness. Surveys, focus groups, or online reviews can help gauge customer perceptions of the promotion. Key questions to consider include:

- Did the promotional pricing influence your decision to purchase?

- How did you perceive the value of the offer?

- What factors contributed to your decision to buy?

Understanding customer sentiment can help businesses refine their promotional strategies and better align them with customer preferences.

3. Profitability Analysis

While driving sales is important, it is equally essential to evaluate the profitability of promotional pricing campaigns. Businesses should analyze the following factors:

- Gross Margin: Assessing the gross margin during the promotional period can help determine whether the increase in sales compensated for the reduced prices.

- Customer Acquisition Cost: Evaluating the cost of acquiring new customers during the promotion can provide insights into the long-term value of the campaign.

- Return on Investment (ROI): Calculating the ROI of the promotional pricing campaign can help businesses assess whether the investment in discounts and marketing efforts yielded a positive return.

Challenges and Considerations

While promotional pricing can be an effective strategy, it is not without its challenges. Businesses must be mindful of several considerations to ensure that promotional pricing does not negatively impact their brand or bottom line:

1. Brand Perception

Frequent promotional pricing can lead to consumer perceptions of a brand as "cheap" or "discounted." This can erode brand equity and make it challenging to maintain premium pricing in the future. Businesses should strike a balance between promotional pricing and maintaining brand value.

2. Customer Expectations

Once customers become accustomed to promotional pricing, they may expect discounts regularly. This can lead to a cycle where customers delay purchases in anticipation of future promotions, ultimately impacting overall sales.

3. Impact on Profit Margins

While promotional pricing can drive short-term sales, it can also squeeze profit margins. Businesses must carefully evaluate the financial implications of discounts to ensure that they do not compromise long-term profitability.

4. Competitive Response

Promotional pricing can trigger competitive responses, leading to a race to the bottom where competitors engage in aggressive discounting. Businesses must be prepared to navigate this landscape and avoid getting caught in a pricing war.

Promotional pricing techniques are a valuable component of a comprehensive pricing strategy, enabling businesses to drive sales, attract new customers, and enhance brand visibility. By designing effective promotional pricing campaigns, understanding target audiences, and measuring the impact of promotions, businesses can leverage this strategy for maximum effectiveness.

However, it is essential to approach promotional pricing thoughtfully, considering the potential impact on brand perception, customer expectations, and profit margins. By balancing the short-term benefits of promotional pricing with long-term brand strategy, businesses can achieve sustainable growth and success in a competitive marketplace.

As we move forward in this book, we will explore other pricing strategies, including discount pricing strategies, to further enhance your understanding of how to master pricing for competitive success.

Chapter 14: Discount Pricing Strategies

Discount pricing strategies are a powerful tool in the arsenal of any business aiming to enhance its market presence, attract new customers, and increase sales volume. However, the effectiveness of discount pricing hinges on a nuanced understanding of its types, applications, and the delicate balance required to maintain brand perception. This chapter delves into the various types of discount pricing, their strategic uses, and the implications for brand equity.

Types of Discount Pricing

Discount pricing can take many forms, each tailored to achieve specific business objectives. Understanding these types is essential for effectively implementing a discount strategy.

1. Seasonal Discounts

Seasonal discounts are typically offered during specific times of the year, such as holidays, back-to-school periods, or end-of-season sales. These discounts encourage consumers to purchase items that may be out of season or to clear inventory. For example, retailers often reduce prices on winter clothing in spring to make way for summer inventory.

Strategic Use: Seasonal discounts can create urgency and encourage customers to make purchases they might otherwise delay. By timing these discounts strategically, businesses can maximize sales during peak shopping periods.

2. Promotional Discounts

Promotional discounts are short-term price reductions designed to stimulate sales during a specific campaign or event. These discounts often accompany new product launches, anniversaries, or special events.

Strategic Use: Promotional discounts can generate buzz and attract attention to a product or service. They are particularly effective in drawing in new customers who may not have considered the brand previously.

3. Volume Discounts

Volume discounts incentivize customers to purchase larger quantities of a product by offering a lower price per unit. This type of discount is common in wholesale and

B2B transactions but can also be applied in retail settings.

Strategic Use: Volume discounts can increase average order size, improve customer loyalty, and reduce inventory costs. They encourage customers to buy more, thus improving cash flow and inventory turnover.

4. Loyalty Discounts

Loyalty discounts reward repeat customers for their continued patronage. These discounts can take the form of points systems, exclusive offers, or percentage reductions on future purchases.

Strategic Use: Loyalty discounts foster customer retention and encourage repeat business. By rewarding loyal customers, businesses can build strong relationships that lead to long-term profitability.

5. Clearance Discounts

Clearance discounts are used to sell off old or excess inventory. These discounts are often deep and are intended to move products quickly to make room for new stock.

Strategic Use: Clearance discounts can help businesses recover costs on unsold inventory while minimizing losses. They are effective in maintaining a fresh product offering and avoiding obsolescence.

6. Referral Discounts

Referral discounts incentivize existing customers to refer new customers. Both the referrer and the new customer typically receive a discount.

Strategic Use: Referral discounts leverage word-of-mouth marketing, which can be a highly effective way to acquire new customers. This strategy not only rewards existing customers but also broadens the customer base.

Balancing Discounts with Brand Perception

While discount pricing can drive sales and attract customers, it is crucial to consider its impact on brand perception. Frequent or deep discounts can lead customers to perceive a brand as low-quality or desperate, potentially harming long-term profitability and brand equity.

1. Understanding Brand Equity

Brand equity refers to the value added to a product or service based on the brand's reputation, recognition, and customer loyalty. A strong brand can command higher prices and create customer loyalty, while a weak brand may struggle to compete on price alone.

2. The Risk of Over-Discounting

Over-reliance on discount pricing can erode brand equity. Customers may come to expect discounts and resist purchasing at full price. This expectation can lead to a cycle of discounting that diminishes perceived value.

Example: A luxury brand that frequently offers discounts may find its products perceived as less exclusive, leading to a decline in desirability and market position.

3. Maintaining Perceived Value

To balance discount pricing with brand perception, businesses should focus on maintaining perceived value. This can be achieved through:

- Communicating Quality: Emphasize the quality and uniqueness of products, even when discounts are offered. Highlighting craftsmanship, materials, or brand heritage can reinforce value.

- Limited-Time Offers: Creating urgency through limited-time discounts can encourage purchases without permanently altering price expectations.

- Bundling Products: Offering discounts on bundled products can provide value without undermining the individual product's perceived worth.

- Exclusive Discounts: Providing discounts to select customer segments, such as loyalty program members, can maintain exclusivity while rewarding loyal customers.

Implementing Discount Pricing Strategies

Implementing discount pricing strategies requires careful planning and execution. Here are some steps to consider:

1. Define Objectives

Before implementing any discount pricing strategy, it is essential to define clear objectives. Are you aiming to increase sales volume, attract new customers, clear inventory, or reward loyalty? Understanding the goal will guide the strategy's design.

2. Analyze Customer Behavior

Understanding customer behavior is critical for effective discount pricing. Analyze purchasing patterns, preferences, and price sensitivity to tailor discounts that resonate with your target audience.

3. Monitor Competitor Strategies

Keeping an eye on competitors' pricing strategies can provide valuable insights. Understanding how competitors use discounts can help you position your own strategies effectively and identify opportunities for differentiation.

4. Test and Measure

Implement discount pricing strategies on a trial basis to measure their effectiveness. Use A/B testing to compare different discount approaches and analyze their impact on sales, customer acquisition, and brand perception.

5. Communicate Clearly

Effective communication is crucial when introducing discount pricing. Ensure that customers understand the terms of the discount, the duration, and any limitations. Clear communication helps manage expectations and reinforces the value of the offer.

Case Studies of Successful Discount Pricing Strategies

To illustrate the effectiveness of discount pricing strategies, let's examine a few real-world examples.

Case Study 1: Amazon Prime Day

Amazon Prime Day is an annual event where the company offers significant discounts exclusively for Prime members. This event not only drives sales but also boosts Prime memberships, creating a win-win scenario.

Analysis: By offering exclusive discounts to a loyal customer base, Amazon reinforces brand loyalty while attracting new customers. The event creates a sense of urgency and excitement, leading to increased sales and customer engagement.

Case Study 2: Starbucks Happy Hour

Starbucks runs a "Happy Hour" promotion where customers can enjoy discounts on select beverages during specific hours. This strategy boosts foot traffic during slower periods and encourages customers to try new products.

Analysis: By creating a limited-time offer, Starbucks effectively increases sales while maintaining its premium brand image. The promotion enhances customer experience and encourages repeat visits.

Case Study 3: Old Navy's Super Cash

Old Navy's Super Cash program allows customers to earn discounts on future purchases based on their spending. This strategy incentivizes higher spending while rewarding loyalty.

Analysis: The Super Cash program encourages customers to return for future purchases, fostering brand loyalty while subtly promoting higher average order values. It strikes a balance between discounting and maintaining perceived value.

Conclusion

Discount pricing strategies can be a powerful means of driving sales and attracting customers, but they require careful consideration to avoid damaging brand perception. By understanding the various types of discounts and their strategic applications, businesses can effectively leverage discount pricing to enhance profitability and market presence.

Balancing discounts with brand equity is crucial. Maintaining perceived value while offering discounts can help ensure long-term success. With clear objectives, a deep understanding of customer behavior, and effective communication, businesses can implement discount pricing strategies that not only drive sales but also reinforce brand loyalty and equity. As the market continues to evolve, mastering discount pricing will remain an essential skill for any business aiming for competitive success.

Chapter 15: Understanding Price Sensitivity

In the intricate world of pricing strategies, understanding price sensitivity is paramount for businesses aiming to optimize their pricing models and ensure maximum profitability. Price sensitivity, or the degree to which the price of a product affects consumers' purchasing behaviors, is influenced by a myriad of factors, including consumer perceptions, market conditions, and the nature of the product itself. This chapter delves into the various factors that influence price sensitivity among consumers and outlines effective strategies to manage it.

Factors Influencing Price Sensitivity

1. Consumer Perceptions of Value

One of the most significant factors affecting price sensitivity is the consumer's perception of value. When consumers believe they are receiving high value for their money, they are less likely to be sensitive to price changes. Conversely, if they perceive a product as overpriced or not offering substantial benefits, even a slight increase in price can deter them from making a purchase.

Example: Luxury brands often maintain a high price point because their consumers perceive the brand as synonymous with quality, exclusivity, and status. These consumers are less price-sensitive because they associate the price with the value of the brand.

2. Availability of Substitutes

The availability of alternative products significantly influences price sensitivity. When consumers have numerous substitutes to choose from, they are more likely to switch to a competitor if prices rise. This is particularly evident in markets with many similar products, where consumers can easily compare prices.

Example: In the fast-food industry, if one chain raises its prices, customers can easily opt for another chain that offers similar menu items at a lower cost, demonstrating high price sensitivity.

3. Income Levels

The income levels of consumers play a crucial role in their price sensitivity. Generally, lower-income consumers tend to be more price-sensitive than higher-income consumers. This is because a price increase may represent a more significant portion of their disposable income, making them more cautious about spending.

Example: During economic downturns, even affluent consumers may exhibit heightened price sensitivity as they reassess their spending habits, indicating that economic conditions can shift price sensitivity across different income brackets.

4. Brand Loyalty

Brand loyalty can reduce price sensitivity. Consumers who are loyal to a brand are often willing to pay a premium for their preferred products, as they trust the brand's quality and value. However, brand loyalty can be fragile; if a competitor offers a compelling alternative, even loyal customers may reconsider their choices.

Example: Apple has cultivated a loyal customer base that is often willing to pay higher prices for its products due to perceived quality and brand prestige. However, if a competitor introduces a product with similar features at a significantly lower price, even loyal customers might reconsider.

5. Market Conditions

Economic factors, such as inflation, unemployment rates, and overall economic stability, can affect price sensitivity. In times of economic uncertainty, consumers tend to be more cautious with their spending, leading to increased price sensitivity.

Example: During a recession, consumers may prioritize essential goods and services, becoming more sensitive to price changes in non-essential items. Businesses must be aware of these market conditions and adjust their pricing strategies accordingly.

6. Product Type

The nature of the product itself also impacts price sensitivity. Necessities tend to have lower price sensitivity compared to luxury items. Consumers are generally less sensitive to price changes for essential goods, as they are less likely to forgo these purchases.

Example: While consumers may be willing to pay a premium for medicine or groceries, they might be more sensitive to price changes for luxury goods like designer handbags or high-end electronics.

Strategies to Manage Price Sensitivity

Understanding the factors influencing price sensitivity allows businesses to implement effective strategies to manage it. Here are some tactics that can be employed:

1. Segmenting the Market

By segmenting the market based on consumer characteristics, businesses can tailor their pricing strategies to different consumer groups. This allows for more precise targeting of price-sensitive customers while maintaining higher prices for less sensitive segments.

Example: A software company might offer different pricing tiers based on the size of the business, providing a lower-priced option for small businesses while maintaining premium pricing for larger enterprises that value additional features and support.

2. Communicating Value

Clearly communicating the value proposition of a product can help mitigate price sensitivity. When consumers understand the benefits and unique features of a product, they are more likely to perceive it as worth the price.

Example: A company launching a new health supplement can emphasize its unique ingredients, scientific backing, and health benefits through targeted marketing campaigns, reinforcing the product's value and justifying its price.

3. Implementing Price Bundling

Price bundling can be an effective way to manage price sensitivity. By grouping products or services together at a discounted rate, businesses can encourage consumers to perceive higher value, making them less sensitive to the individual prices.

Example: A telecommunications provider might offer a bundle that includes internet, cable, and phone services at a lower combined price than purchasing each service separately, making the overall package more attractive to price-sensitive consumers.

4. Utilizing Psychological Pricing

Psychological pricing strategies, such as charm pricing (e.g., pricing a product at $9.99 instead of $10.00), can influence consumer perception and reduce price sensitivity. These strategies play on consumer psychology and can make prices appear more attractive.

Example: Retailers often use charm pricing to create the illusion of a bargain, leading consumers to view the price as significantly lower than it is, thus reducing their sensitivity to price increases.

5. Offering Flexible Payment Options

Providing flexible payment options, such as installment

plans or financing, can help manage price sensitivity. When consumers can spread the cost of a purchase over time, they may be less deterred by higher prices.

Example: Furniture retailers often offer financing plans that allow customers to pay for their purchases over several months, making it easier for price-sensitive consumers to afford higher-priced items.

6. Monitoring Competitors' Pricing Strategies

Keeping a close eye on competitors' pricing strategies can help businesses remain competitive and responsive to market changes. By understanding how competitors price similar products, businesses can adjust their own pricing strategies to manage price sensitivity effectively.

Example: A travel company may monitor competitors' pricing for vacation packages and adjust its own prices or offer promotions to attract price-sensitive customers during peak travel seasons.

7. Testing and Experimentation

Conducting pricing experiments can provide valuable insights into price sensitivity. A/B testing different price points or promotional offers can help businesses identify the optimal pricing strategy that maximizes sales without alienating price-sensitive consumers.

Example: An e-commerce platform might test different pricing strategies for a popular product, analyzing sales data to determine which price point yields the highest revenue while maintaining customer satisfaction.

Conclusion

Understanding price sensitivity is crucial for businesses striving to optimize their pricing strategies and enhance profitability. By recognizing the factors that influence price sensitivity, such as consumer perceptions of value, availability of substitutes, income levels, brand loyalty, market conditions, and product type, businesses can develop targeted strategies to manage it effectively.

Implementing strategies such as market segmentation, value communication, price bundling, psychological pricing, flexible payment options, competitive monitoring, and testing can help businesses navigate the complexities of price sensitivity. Ultimately, mastering the nuances of price sensitivity is essential for achieving competitive success in today's dynamic market landscape. As businesses continue to refine their pricing strategies, they will be better positioned to meet the needs of their customers while maximizing profitability and market dominance.

Chapter 16: Price Positioning in the Market

In the competitive landscape of modern business, price positioning is not merely about setting a number; it is a strategic endeavor that encompasses a brand's identity, perceived value, and market segment. This chapter delves into the intricacies of defining your brand's price positioning and offers actionable strategies to communicate that positioning effectively to your target audience.

Understanding Price Positioning

Price positioning refers to the strategic placement of your product or service within the market based on its pricing relative to competitors and its perceived value by consumers. It is an essential aspect of your overall marketing strategy, as it influences consumer perception, competitive advantage, and ultimately, profitability.

When a company clearly defines its price positioning, it

can articulate the value it offers to consumers, justify its pricing strategy, and differentiate itself from competitors. This differentiation is crucial in crowded markets where consumers have numerous options. Effective price positioning can create a unique identity for a brand, leading to customer loyalty and increased market share.

The Importance of Price Positioning

1. Consumer Perception: Price is often a direct reflection of quality in the eyes of consumers. A well-positioned price can signal premium quality, while a lower price might suggest value or affordability. Understanding how your target market perceives price is critical in establishing the right positioning.

2. Competitive Advantage: In a saturated market, price positioning can provide a competitive edge. By positioning your product at a strategic price point, you can attract specific customer segments who are willing to pay for perceived value or who are looking for the best deal.

3. Market Segmentation: Different customer segments have varying price sensitivities and perceptions of value. Price positioning allows you to tailor your offerings to meet the needs of distinct market segments, optimizing your reach and impact.

4. Brand Identity: Price positioning is integral to your brand's identity. Whether you aim to be viewed as a luxury brand or a budget-friendly option, your pricing strategy must align with your overall branding efforts to create a cohesive message.

Defining Your Brand's Price Positioning

To effectively define your brand's price positioning, consider the following steps:

1. Analyze Your Market

Begin by conducting thorough market research to understand the competitive landscape. Identify key competitors, their pricing strategies, and how they position themselves in the market. This analysis will provide insights into potential pricing tiers and market gaps that your brand can exploit.

2. Understand Your Target Audience

Your target audience is at the heart of your price positioning strategy. Conduct surveys, focus groups, or interviews to gather information about their preferences, purchasing behaviors, and price sensitivities. Understanding what drives their purchasing decisions will help you tailor your pricing strategy to meet their needs.

3. Evaluate Your Value Proposition

Your value proposition is the unique value your product or service offers to customers. Evaluate how your offerings compare to those of competitors in terms of features, benefits, and overall value. This assessment will help you determine where you can position your price relative to the perceived value.

4. Choose Your Pricing Strategy

Based on your market analysis, audience understanding, and value proposition evaluation, select a pricing strategy that aligns with your brand's goals. This could include premium pricing, competitive pricing, penetration pricing, or value-based pricing, among others. Ensure that your chosen strategy reflects the brand image you wish to convey.

5. Test and Adjust

Once you have defined your price positioning, it is essential to test it in the market. Launch your product or service at the chosen price point and monitor customer feedback, sales performance, and competitive reactions. Be prepared to adjust your pricing strategy based on real-world results and changing market conditions.

Strategies to Communicate Price Positioning Effectively

Once you have established your price positioning, the

next step is to communicate it effectively to your target audience. Here are several strategies to achieve this:

1. Craft a Compelling Brand Story

Your brand story should reflect your values, mission, and the unique benefits of your product or service. By weaving your price positioning into your brand narrative, you can create an emotional connection with consumers that reinforces the value of your pricing strategy. For example, if you are positioning as a premium brand, highlight the craftsmanship, quality materials, and exclusive experiences associated with your offerings.

2. Utilize Marketing Channels Wisely

Choose the right marketing channels to reach your target audience effectively. Social media, email marketing, content marketing, and traditional advertising can all play a role in communicating your price positioning. Tailor your messaging to each channel while maintaining consistency in your overall branding.

3. Leverage Customer Testimonials and Reviews

Customer testimonials and reviews can significantly influence potential buyers' perceptions of value. Encourage satisfied customers to share their experiences and highlight how your product or service justifies its price. Authentic feedback can reinforce your price positioning and build trust with prospective customers.

4. Offer Transparent Pricing

Transparency in pricing can enhance consumer trust and confidence in your brand. Clearly communicate what is included in the price, any additional costs, and the value that customers receive. Avoid hidden fees or complex pricing structures that may lead to confusion or frustration.

5. Create Value-Added Content

Providing educational content that highlights the benefits and features of your product or service can reinforce your price positioning. Create blog posts, videos, infographics, or webinars that demonstrate the value your offerings provide. This approach not only positions your brand as an authority but also justifies the pricing strategy.

Case Studies of Successful Price Positioning

To illustrate the effectiveness of price positioning, let's explore a few case studies of companies that have successfully defined and communicated their price positioning in the market.

Case Study 1: Apple Inc.

Apple is a prime example of successful price positioning. The company positions itself as a premium brand, offering high-quality products at higher price points than many competitors. Apple's marketing emphasizes design, innovation, and user experience, reinforcing the perception of value that justifies its pricing. The brand story, combined with sleek advertising and a dedicated customer base, has allowed Apple to maintain its premium pricing strategy while achieving immense profitability.

Case Study 2: Walmart

Walmart's price positioning strategy focuses on being the low-cost leader in retail. The company communicates this positioning through its "Everyday Low Prices" slogan, which emphasizes affordability and value. Walmart's marketing efforts highlight price comparisons and savings, appealing to budget-conscious consumers. By consistently delivering on its promise of low prices, Walmart has solidified its position as a go-to destination for value-driven shoppers.

Case Study 3: Tesla

Tesla has positioned itself as a leader in electric vehicles with an emphasis on innovation and sustainability. While its vehicles are priced higher than traditional cars, Tesla effectively communicates the long-term savings associated with electric vehicles, such as reduced fuel and maintenance costs. The brand's commitment to cutting-edge technology and environmental responsibility appeals to consumers willing to invest in a premium product that aligns with their values.

Challenges in Price Positioning

While defining and communicating price positioning is essential for success, businesses may encounter several challenges:

1. Market Fluctuations: Changes in the market, such as economic downturns or shifts in consumer preferences, can impact price positioning. Companies must remain agile and be prepared to adjust their strategies accordingly.

2. Competitive Pressures: Competitors may react to your pricing strategy by altering their own prices or enhancing their value propositions. It is crucial to monitor the competitive landscape continuously and adapt your positioning as needed.

3. Consumer Perceptions: Consumer perceptions can be influenced by external factors, such as social media or economic conditions. Maintaining a positive brand image and effectively managing public relations is vital to

sustaining price positioning.

4. Internal Alignment: Ensuring that all departments within the organization understand and support the price positioning strategy is essential. Marketing, sales, and product development teams must work collaboratively to present a unified message to consumers.

Conclusion

Price positioning is a critical component of a successful pricing strategy. By carefully defining your brand's price positioning and communicating it effectively, you can influence consumer perception, gain a competitive advantage, and drive profitability. Remember that price positioning is not a one-time effort; it requires continuous evaluation and adaptation to remain relevant in an ever-changing market. By staying attuned to consumer needs and market dynamics, your brand can achieve lasting success through effective price positioning.

Chapter 17: Price Negotiation Skills

In the ever-evolving landscape of business, the ability to negotiate prices effectively can be a game-changer. Price negotiation is not merely a transactional process; it is an art that intertwines psychology, strategy, and relationship-building. This chapter delves into the essential skills and techniques for effective price negotiation, emphasizing the importance of building relationships through negotiation processes. By mastering these skills, you will be better equipped to secure favorable terms while fostering long-lasting partnerships.

Understanding the Foundations of Price Negotiation

Before diving into negotiation techniques, it is vital to understand the foundational elements that contribute to successful price negotiations. The essence of negotiation lies in the ability to reach an agreement that satisfies both parties. This requires a clear understanding of your objectives, the value you bring to the table, and the needs and motivations of the other party.

1. Preparation is Key: The first step in any negotiation is thorough preparation. This involves researching the market, understanding your product's value proposition, and knowing your competitor's pricing structures. Additionally, it is crucial to define your bottom line—the minimum price you are willing to accept—and your target price, which is the ideal outcome of the negotiation.

2. Know Your Value: Articulating the value of your product or service is essential in negotiations. You must be able to convey not only the features of what you are offering but also the benefits that set it apart from competitors. This could include unique selling propositions, superior service, or additional benefits that justify your pricing.

3. Understand the Other Party's Perspective: Empathy plays a significant role in negotiations. Understanding the motivations, constraints, and objectives of the other party can help you tailor your approach. This insight allows you to identify potential win-win scenarios where both parties feel they have gained value.

Techniques for Effective Price Negotiation

Having established a foundation, it is time to explore specific techniques that can enhance your negotiation skills. These techniques range from communication strategies to psychological tactics that can influence the outcome of negotiations.

1. Building Rapport: Establishing a positive relationship with the other party can significantly impact the negotiation process. Begin by finding common ground and engaging in small talk to create a comfortable atmosphere. When both parties feel at ease, they are more likely to collaborate and reach an agreement.

2. Active Listening: Listening is a powerful tool in negotiations. By actively listening to the other party, you can gain valuable insights into their needs and concerns. This not only demonstrates respect but also allows you to adjust your approach based on their feedback. Repeat back what you have heard to confirm understanding and show that you value their perspective.

3. Framing the Discussion: How you frame your proposal can influence the other party's perception of the negotiation. Instead of presenting your price as a fixed number, frame it in terms of value. For example, instead of saying, "Our product costs $X," you might say, "For an investment of $X, you will receive [list benefits], which will ultimately lead to [positive outcome]." This approach shifts the focus from price to value.

4. Using Anchoring: Anchoring is a psychological tactic where you set a reference point for the negotiation. By presenting a higher initial price, you create a benchmark that can make subsequent offers appear more reasonable. However, be cautious with this technique; if your anchor is too high, it may deter the other party from engaging further.

5. Employing Concessions Strategically: Concessions are a natural part of negotiation, but they should be made strategically. When you make a concession, do so in a way that emphasizes the value of what you are giving up. For example, if you lower your price, you might also highlight additional benefits or services that you will provide at that price. This reinforces the idea that the negotiation is a collaborative effort rather than a zero-sum game.

6. Creating Urgency: Introducing a sense of urgency can motivate the other party to make a decision more quickly. This could be achieved by highlighting limited-time offers, inventory constraints, or upcoming price increases. However, use this tactic sparingly and ethically, as excessive pressure can lead to resentment and damage relationships.

Building Relationships Through Negotiation

While price negotiation often focuses on immediate

outcomes, it is essential to view it as an opportunity to build long-term relationships. Strong relationships can lead to repeat business, referrals, and collaborative opportunities that extend beyond the initial negotiation.

1. Follow Up: After a negotiation concludes, follow up with the other party to express appreciation for their time and consideration. This gesture reinforces the relationship and opens the door for future interactions. Additionally, checking in after the sale to ensure satisfaction can lead to positive word-of-mouth and repeat business.

2. Be Transparent: Transparency fosters trust in negotiations. Being open about your pricing structure, the rationale behind your offers, and any constraints you face can help build credibility. When the other party feels they understand your position, they are more likely to engage in a fair and constructive negotiation.

3. Seek Feedback: After a negotiation, consider soliciting feedback from the other party regarding their experience. This not only shows that you value their opinion but also provides you with insights to improve your negotiation skills in the future. Moreover, it demonstrates your commitment to continuous improvement and relationship-building.

Overcoming Common Negotiation Challenges

Price negotiations can be fraught with challenges, from differing expectations to emotional responses. Here are some common challenges and strategies to overcome them:

1. Dealing with Objections: It is common for the other party to raise objections during negotiations. Instead of viewing objections as roadblocks, consider them opportunities to clarify misunderstandings and address concerns. Acknowledge their objections and respond with data, testimonials, or additional information that reinforces your value proposition.

2. Managing Emotions: Emotions can run high during negotiations, particularly when price is a sensitive topic. Maintain your composure and professionalism, even if the other party becomes emotional. Practicing mindfulness techniques, such as deep breathing or pausing before responding, can help you stay calm and focused.

3. Handling Difficult Personalities: Negotiating with individuals who are aggressive or confrontational can be challenging. In such cases, it is essential to remain assertive while avoiding escalation. Use techniques such as active listening and reframing to steer the

conversation back to productive dialogue. If necessary, consider taking a break to allow tempers to cool before resuming negotiations.

Conclusion: The Art of Price Negotiation

Mastering price negotiation skills is crucial for achieving competitive success in today's market. By understanding the foundations of negotiation, employing effective techniques, and prioritizing relationship-building, you can enhance your negotiation outcomes and foster long-term partnerships.

As you continue to develop your negotiation skills, remember that practice is key. Engage in mock negotiations, seek feedback, and reflect on your experiences to refine your approach continually. In doing so, you will unlock the potential for greater profitability and market dominance, positioning yourself as a formidable player in your industry.

In the next chapter, we will explore the critical aspect of communicating pricing effectively, ensuring that your pricing strategies resonate with your target audience and overcome any objections they may have.

Chapter 18: Communicating Pricing Effectively

In an increasingly competitive marketplace, where consumers are more informed and discerning than ever, the ability to communicate pricing effectively is paramount. Pricing is not merely a number; it is a message that conveys value, quality, and positioning. This chapter delves into the strategies for clear price communication and addresses how to overcome pricing objections from customers. By mastering these elements, businesses can enhance their pricing strategies and foster stronger relationships with their customers.

The Importance of Clear Price Communication

Effective communication of pricing is crucial for several reasons:

1. Establishing Trust: Transparent pricing builds trust with customers. When consumers understand what they are paying for and why, they are more likely to feel confident

in their purchase decisions.

2. Enhancing Value Perception: Clear communication helps to articulate the value proposition of a product or service. When customers comprehend the benefits and features associated with a price, they are more inclined to perceive it as justified.

3. Reducing Pricing Objections: A well-communicated price can preemptively address potential objections. By anticipating concerns and responding to them in advance, businesses can mitigate resistance and foster a smoother sales process.

4. Facilitating Decision-Making: Clear pricing information simplifies the decision-making process for consumers. When prices are straightforward and easy to understand, customers can make quicker, more informed choices.

5. Differentiating from Competitors: In a crowded market, effective price communication can set a brand apart. By clearly articulating the reasons behind pricing strategies, businesses can highlight their unique selling propositions.

Strategies for Clear Price Communication

To communicate pricing effectively, businesses should consider the following strategies:

1. Use Simple Language

Avoid jargon or overly complex terms when discussing pricing. Use straightforward language that is easily understood by your target audience. For instance, instead of saying "our premium package includes a comprehensive suite of services," you might say "our premium package gives you everything you need to succeed, including personalized support and exclusive resources."

2. Provide Context

Contextualizing pricing helps customers understand the rationale behind it. For example, if a product is priced higher than competitors, explain the reasons—such as superior quality, unique features, or exceptional customer service. Providing context can help justify the price and enhance perceived value.

3. Highlight Value Over Cost

Shift the focus from the cost to the value offered. Instead of emphasizing the price tag, highlight the benefits and outcomes that the customer will receive. For instance, instead of saying "this service costs $500," you might say "for just $500, you'll gain access to our expert team and resources that will save you time and increase your revenue."

4. Use Visual Aids

Visual aids can enhance understanding and retention. Use charts, graphs, or infographics to illustrate pricing structures, comparisons, or value propositions. Visual representations can make complex pricing models more digestible and engaging.

5. Be Transparent About Pricing Changes

If prices need to change due to market conditions or other factors, communicate these changes transparently. Explain the reasons for the adjustment and how it aligns with the value provided. Transparency fosters trust and helps customers feel more comfortable with the changes.

6. Create a Pricing FAQ

Develop a Frequently Asked Questions (FAQ) section on your website or marketing materials that addresses common pricing concerns. This can include information about payment plans, discounts, or hidden fees. An FAQ can serve as a valuable resource for customers and reduce the burden on sales teams.

7. Train Your Team

Ensure that your sales and customer service teams are well-versed in pricing communication. Provide training on how to effectively convey pricing information and respond to objections. A knowledgeable team can instill confidence in customers and enhance the overall customer experience.

Overcoming Pricing Objections

Despite best efforts in communicating pricing, objections may still arise. Here are strategies to effectively address and overcome these objections:

1. Listen Actively

When a customer raises a pricing objection, listen carefully to understand their concerns. Active listening demonstrates empathy and allows you to address the specific issue at hand. Avoid interrupting and ensure that the customer feels heard.

2. Acknowledge the Concern

Recognizing the customer's concern is crucial. A simple acknowledgment can diffuse tension and show that you value their opinion. For example, you might say, "I understand that the price seems higher than you expected."

3. Provide Justification

After acknowledging the concern, provide justification for the pricing. Use the context established earlier to explain why the price is set at that level. Highlight the unique value and benefits that justify the cost.

4. Offer Alternatives

If a customer is resistant to a particular price point, consider offering alternatives. This could include different pricing tiers, discounts for bulk purchases, or payment plans. Providing options can help meet the customer's needs while still aligning with your pricing strategy.

5. Share Testimonials and Case Studies

Leverage social proof to overcome objections. Share testimonials from satisfied customers or case studies that demonstrate the value of your product or service. Hearing positive experiences from others can help alleviate concerns about pricing.

6. Focus on Long-Term Value

Encourage customers to consider the long-term value of their investment. Highlight how your product or service can save them money, time, or resources in the future. Shifting the focus from short-term cost to long-term benefit can help justify the price.

7. Be Prepared to Walk Away

In some cases, a customer may remain unwilling to accept

the pricing. While it's important to be flexible, it's equally important to recognize when to stand firm. If the price is justified and the customer is not willing to see the value, be prepared to walk away. This can sometimes create a sense of urgency or prompt the customer to reconsider.

Conclusion

Communicating pricing effectively is an essential skill for businesses seeking to enhance their competitive edge. By employing clear communication strategies and proactively addressing pricing objections, organizations can foster trust, enhance value perception, and ultimately drive sales. As the marketplace continues to evolve, mastering the art of pricing communication will be a critical component of successful pricing strategies.

In the next chapter, we will explore the role of pricing analytics in decision-making, providing insights into how data-driven approaches can optimize pricing strategies for better outcomes.

Chapter 19: Pricing Analytics for Decision Making

In today's highly competitive business landscape, where every decision can significantly impact profitability, the importance of data-driven decision-making cannot be overstated. Pricing analytics has emerged as a critical component of pricing strategy, enabling organizations to leverage data to make informed pricing decisions that enhance profitability and market positioning. This chapter delves into the intricacies of pricing analytics, exploring its role in decision-making, the tools and techniques available, and the best practices for integrating analytics into pricing strategies.

The Role of Pricing Analytics in Decision Making

Pricing analytics involves the systematic analysis of data related to pricing strategies and market dynamics. It encompasses various methodologies and tools that help organizations understand consumer behavior, market trends, and competitive pricing structures. The insights gained from pricing analytics empower businesses to make strategic decisions that align pricing with overall business objectives.

1. Understanding Market Dynamics: Pricing analytics provides insights into how market fluctuations, consumer preferences, and competitive actions influence pricing strategies. By analyzing historical data and market trends, businesses can anticipate changes in demand and adjust their pricing accordingly.

2. Enhancing Customer Segmentation: Effective pricing analytics allows organizations to segment their customer base more accurately. By understanding the price sensitivity and purchasing behavior of different segments, businesses can tailor their pricing strategies to meet the unique needs of each group.

3. Optimizing Price Points: Through advanced analytics, companies can identify the optimal price points for their products or services. This involves analyzing various pricing scenarios and their potential impact on sales volume, revenue, and profitability.

4. Forecasting Demand: Pricing analytics enables businesses to forecast demand more accurately. By analyzing historical sales data and external market

factors, organizations can predict future sales trends and adjust their pricing strategies to maximize revenue.

5. Evaluating Pricing Strategies: Organizations can assess the effectiveness of their pricing strategies through analytics. By measuring key performance indicators (KPIs) such as sales growth, profit margins, and customer acquisition costs, businesses can determine which pricing strategies are yielding the best results.

Tools and Techniques for Pricing Analytics

To harness the power of pricing analytics, organizations must utilize a variety of tools and techniques. Here, we explore some of the most effective pricing analytics tools available today.

1. Data Visualization Tools

Data visualization tools such as Tableau, Power BI, and Google Data Studio allow organizations to transform complex data sets into intuitive visual representations. These tools help stakeholders quickly grasp pricing trends, customer behavior, and market dynamics, facilitating faster and more informed decision-making.

2. Statistical Analysis Software

Statistical analysis software like R and Python's Pandas library enables businesses to conduct detailed statistical analyses on pricing data. These tools can help organizations understand correlations between pricing changes and sales performance, as well as identify outliers and trends within the data.

3. Predictive Analytics

Predictive analytics tools, such as SAS and IBM Watson, allow organizations to forecast future pricing trends based on historical data. By employing machine learning algorithms, these tools can identify patterns in consumer behavior and market conditions, enabling businesses to make proactive pricing decisions.

4. Price Optimization Software

Price optimization software, such as Pricefx and Vendavo, provides organizations with the capabilities to test various pricing scenarios and identify the optimal price points for their products. These tools often incorporate advanced algorithms that consider factors such as demand elasticity, competitive pricing, and customer preferences.

5. Customer Relationship Management (CRM) Systems

CRM systems like Salesforce and HubSpot can be

integrated with pricing analytics tools to provide a comprehensive view of customer interactions and sales performance. By analyzing customer data alongside pricing information, organizations can better understand how pricing affects customer behavior and loyalty.

Best Practices for Integrating Pricing Analytics into Decision Making

To effectively leverage pricing analytics, organizations should adopt best practices that ensure data-driven decision-making becomes an integral part of their pricing strategy.

1. Establish Clear Objectives

Before diving into pricing analytics, organizations must establish clear objectives for what they hope to achieve. Whether the goal is to increase market share, enhance profitability, or improve customer retention, having a defined objective will guide the analytics process and ensure that insights are aligned with business goals.

2. Invest in Data Quality

The effectiveness of pricing analytics is heavily dependent on the quality of the data being analyzed. Organizations should invest in data collection methods that ensure accuracy and completeness. This includes regularly cleaning and updating data sets, as well as implementing robust data governance practices.

3. Foster a Data-Driven Culture

To fully realize the benefits of pricing analytics, organizations must foster a data-driven culture. This involves encouraging employees at all levels to embrace data analysis and use insights to inform their decision-making. Training and resources should be provided to equip teams with the skills necessary to interpret and act on data findings.

4. Collaborate Across Departments

Pricing decisions often involve multiple departments, including marketing, sales, finance, and operations. To ensure a holistic approach to pricing analytics, organizations should promote cross-functional collaboration. This can be achieved through regular meetings and workshops that bring together representatives from different departments to share insights and align on pricing strategies.

5. Continuously Monitor and Adjust

Pricing analytics is not a one-time exercise; it requires continuous monitoring and adjustment. Organizations should regularly review their pricing strategies in light of new data and market changes. This iterative approach allows businesses to remain agile and responsive to evolving consumer preferences and competitive pressures.

Case Studies in Pricing Analytics

To illustrate the power of pricing analytics in decision-making, let's examine a few case studies of organizations that successfully integrated analytics into their pricing strategies.

Case Study 1: Retail Giant's Dynamic Pricing Strategy

A leading retail giant implemented a dynamic pricing strategy using advanced analytics to optimize pricing in real-time based on demand fluctuations and competitor pricing. By leveraging data from various sources, including sales history, customer behavior, and external market conditions, the retailer was able to adjust prices dynamically.

As a result, the company saw a significant increase in sales, particularly during peak shopping seasons. The use of predictive analytics allowed them to anticipate customer demand more accurately, leading to improved inventory management and reduced markdowns.

Case Study 2: SaaS Company's Value-Based Pricing Model

A Software as a Service (SaaS) company utilized pricing analytics to transition from a cost-based pricing model to a value-based pricing strategy. By analyzing customer feedback, usage data, and competitive offerings, the company identified the unique value propositions of its product.

Through this analysis, the SaaS provider was able to segment its customers based on willingness to pay and tailor pricing packages accordingly. This resulted in a 30% increase in average revenue per user and improved customer satisfaction, as clients felt they were receiving greater value for their investment.

Case Study 3: Airline's Revenue Management System

An international airline implemented a sophisticated revenue management system that utilized pricing analytics to optimize ticket pricing across various routes. By analyzing historical booking data, competitor pricing, and market demand, the airline developed algorithms that adjusted ticket prices in real-time based on supply and demand dynamics.

The implementation of this pricing analytics strategy led to a significant increase in revenue, particularly during peak travel periods. The airline's ability to forecast demand and adjust prices accordingly allowed it to maximize seat occupancy and overall profitability.

Conclusion

In conclusion, pricing analytics is a powerful tool that can significantly enhance decision-making in pricing strategies. By leveraging data-driven insights, organizations can optimize their pricing models, understand market dynamics, and enhance customer segmentation. The integration of advanced analytics tools and techniques, combined with best practices for data management and cross-functional collaboration, will empower businesses to make informed pricing decisions that drive profitability and competitive advantage.

As the business landscape continues to evolve, the role of pricing analytics will only become more critical. Organizations that embrace data-driven decision-making in their pricing strategies will be better equipped to navigate market challenges, respond to consumer behavior, and ultimately achieve sustained success in their pricing endeavors.

Chapter 20: Pricing Optimization Techniques

In the ever-evolving landscape of business, pricing optimization has emerged as a critical component for achieving competitive success. Organizations are increasingly recognizing that effective pricing strategies can significantly impact profitability, market share, and customer loyalty. This chapter delves into the various methods for continuous pricing optimization, supported by real-world case studies that illustrate successful implementations.

Understanding Pricing Optimization

Pricing optimization refers to the process of adjusting prices to maximize revenue while considering factors such as demand, competition, and customer behavior. This dynamic process involves leveraging data analytics, market research, and consumer insights to determine the optimal price point for products and services. The goal is to find a balance between attracting customers and maximizing profit margins.

The Importance of Continuous Optimization

In today's fast-paced business environment, static pricing strategies are no longer sufficient. Market conditions, consumer preferences, and competitive landscapes are constantly changing, necessitating a proactive approach to pricing. Continuous optimization allows businesses to respond swiftly to these changes, ensuring that pricing remains aligned with market realities.

Methods for Continuous Pricing Optimization

1. Data-Driven Decision Making

The foundation of effective pricing optimization lies in data analytics. Organizations must collect and analyze data related to sales, customer behavior, and market trends. By utilizing advanced analytics tools, businesses can uncover patterns and insights that inform pricing decisions.

- Sales Data Analysis: Monitoring sales trends over time helps identify which products are performing well and which are underperforming. This information can guide pricing adjustments to boost sales of lagging products.

- Customer Segmentation: Understanding different

customer segments and their willingness to pay allows for more tailored pricing strategies. For instance, premium customers may be less price-sensitive, enabling businesses to implement higher price points for exclusive offerings.

2. A/B Testing for Pricing Strategies

A/B testing, or split testing, is a powerful method for evaluating the effectiveness of different pricing strategies. By offering two variations of a product at different price points to different customer segments, businesses can measure the impact on sales and revenue.

- Example: An online retailer might test two price points for the same product: one at $49.99 and another at $59.99. By tracking conversion rates and total revenue generated from each price point, the retailer can determine the optimal price that maximizes sales.

3. Competitive Benchmarking

Regularly assessing competitors' pricing strategies is essential for maintaining a competitive edge. By understanding how similar products are priced in the market, businesses can adjust their pricing to remain attractive to consumers without sacrificing profitability.

- Market Positioning: If competitors are offering similar

products at lower prices, a business may need to reevaluate its pricing strategy. This could involve enhancing the perceived value of its offerings through improved marketing or product features.

4. Dynamic Pricing Models

Dynamic pricing involves adjusting prices in real-time based on market demand, competition, and other external factors. This strategy is particularly effective in industries such as travel, hospitality, and e-commerce, where demand fluctuates frequently.

- Algorithmic Pricing: Many businesses employ algorithms that automatically adjust prices based on predefined criteria. For example, an airline may increase ticket prices as the departure date approaches and seats become limited.

5. Customer Feedback and Surveys

Engaging customers through feedback and surveys provides valuable insights into their perceptions of pricing. Understanding how customers view pricing in relation to the value received can inform pricing adjustments.

- Value Perception: If customers perceive a product as being too expensive relative to its benefits, businesses can consider lowering the price or enhancing the product's features to justify the cost.

Case Studies on Successful Pricing Optimization

Case Study 1: Starbucks

Starbucks is renowned for its premium pricing strategy, which reflects the brand's positioning as a high-quality coffee provider. However, the company continuously optimizes its pricing based on various factors, including location, customer preferences, and seasonal trends.

- Implementation of Dynamic Pricing: Starbucks employs a dynamic pricing model in certain markets, adjusting prices based on demand and competition. For instance, during peak hours, prices may be slightly higher to capitalize on increased foot traffic.

- Customer Loyalty Programs: The introduction of the Starbucks Rewards program has further enhanced pricing optimization. By offering personalized discounts and promotions to loyal customers, Starbucks can maintain customer engagement while optimizing revenue.

Case Study 2: Amazon

Amazon's pricing strategy is a prime example of effective pricing optimization through data analytics and dynamic pricing. The company continuously monitors competitor prices and adjusts its own in real-time to ensure competitiveness.

- Algorithmic Pricing: Amazon uses sophisticated algorithms to analyze market conditions and customer behavior, enabling it to adjust prices on millions of products within seconds. This strategy has helped Amazon maintain its position as a market leader.

- Customer-Centric Approach: By leveraging customer data, Amazon tailors pricing strategies to individual preferences, offering personalized discounts and recommendations based on previous purchases.

Challenges in Pricing Optimization

While pricing optimization offers numerous benefits, it is not without challenges. Organizations must navigate several obstacles to ensure successful implementation:

1. Data Quality and Accessibility

The effectiveness of pricing optimization relies heavily on the quality and accessibility of data. Inaccurate or incomplete data can lead to misguided pricing decisions. Businesses must invest in robust data collection and analysis systems to ensure reliable insights.

2. Market Volatility

Rapid changes in market conditions can complicate pricing optimization efforts. Economic downturns, shifts in consumer behavior, and emerging competitors can all impact pricing strategies. Organizations must remain agile and adaptable to respond to these fluctuations.

3. Internal Resistance

Implementing new pricing strategies may encounter resistance from internal stakeholders, particularly if it involves significant changes to established practices. Effective communication and training are essential to foster buy-in and ensure alignment across teams.

Best Practices for Effective Pricing Optimization

To successfully implement pricing optimization techniques, organizations should consider the following best practices:

1. Foster a Data-Driven Culture

Encouraging a culture that values data-driven decision-making is essential for effective pricing optimization. Teams should be trained to leverage data analytics tools and interpret insights to inform pricing strategies.

2. Monitor Competitors Regularly

Establishing a routine for competitive benchmarking

ensures that businesses remain informed about market trends and competitor pricing strategies. Regular assessments can help identify opportunities for pricing adjustments.

3. Engage with Customers

Actively seeking customer feedback and insights can inform pricing strategies and enhance customer satisfaction. Organizations should implement mechanisms for collecting feedback and analyzing customer sentiment regarding pricing.

4. Invest in Technology

Utilizing advanced analytics tools and pricing software can streamline the pricing optimization process. Organizations should invest in technology that facilitates data analysis, dynamic pricing, and customer segmentation.

Conclusion

Pricing optimization is a vital component of a successful pricing strategy. By employing data-driven decision-making, A/B testing, competitive benchmarking, dynamic pricing models, and customer feedback, businesses can continuously refine their pricing strategies to maximize profitability and market share. The case studies of

Starbucks and Amazon illustrate the effectiveness of these techniques in real-world scenarios.

As organizations navigate the complexities of pricing optimization, they must remain adaptable and responsive to market changes. By fostering a culture of continuous improvement and leveraging technology, businesses can unlock the full potential of their pricing strategies, ensuring long-term success in a competitive marketplace.

In the next chapter, we will explore the leadership aspects of pricing strategy development, focusing on how to build a cross-functional team that drives pricing success.

Chapter 21: Leading Your Team in Pricing Strategy Development

In today's fast-paced business environment, effective pricing strategies are not formulated in isolation. They require a collaborative approach that leverages the diverse expertise of various departments within an organization. This chapter will delve into the importance of building a cross-functional team dedicated to pricing strategy development and the leadership skills necessary to guide such a team towards achieving pricing excellence.

Building a Cross-Functional Team for Pricing Success

A cross-functional team consists of members from different departments such as marketing, finance, sales, product development, and customer service. Each member brings unique insights and perspectives that enrich the pricing strategy process. A successful pricing strategy must consider various factors, including market demand, production costs, competitive landscape, and customer psychology. Therefore, the composition of your pricing team should reflect this complexity.

1. Identifying Key Roles and Responsibilities

To build an effective cross-functional team, first identify the key roles that need to be filled:

- Pricing Analyst: Responsible for analyzing data related to pricing models, market trends, and competitive pricing. This role is crucial for providing the quantitative backbone of pricing strategies.

 - Marketing Manager: This person will offer insights into consumer behavior, brand positioning, and promotional strategies. Their understanding of market segmentation is vital for tailoring pricing strategies to different customer groups.

 - Sales Representative: Sales personnel have firsthand knowledge of customer interactions and feedback. Their input can help the team understand how pricing affects sales performance and customer satisfaction.

 - Finance Manager: This role ensures that pricing strategies align with the company's financial goals and constraints. They provide essential insights into cost structures, profit margins, and revenue projections.

- Product Manager: Responsible for understanding the product's lifecycle and features, the product manager can help determine how pricing should evolve as the product matures in the market.

By clearly defining roles, each team member understands their responsibilities and how they contribute to the larger objective of developing effective pricing strategies.

2. Fostering Collaboration and Communication

Once the team is established, fostering an environment of collaboration and open communication is essential. Here are strategies to encourage teamwork:

- Regular Meetings: Schedule consistent team meetings to discuss progress, share insights, and brainstorm new ideas. These meetings should encourage participation from all members, allowing for a diverse range of opinions and suggestions.

 - Shared Goals: Establish common objectives that align with the overall business strategy. When team members understand how their contributions impact the company's success, they are more likely to be engaged and motivated.

 - Collaborative Tools: Utilize project management tools and communication platforms to facilitate information sharing and collaboration. Tools like Slack, Trello, or Asana can help streamline workflows and keep everyone on the same page.

3. Encouraging Innovation and Creativity

Pricing strategy development requires innovative thinking. Encourage your team to think outside the box by:

- Brainstorming Sessions: Organize brainstorming sessions where team members can freely share ideas without fear of criticism. This can lead to creative solutions that may not have been considered otherwise.

 - Encouraging Risk-Taking: Create a culture where calculated risk-taking is encouraged. Allow team members to experiment with new pricing models or strategies, even if they might not succeed. Learning from failures can lead to valuable insights.

- Recognizing Contributions: Acknowledge and reward innovative ideas and contributions. This recognition can motivate team members to continue pushing boundaries and exploring new possibilities.

Leadership Skills for Effective Pricing Management

Leading a cross-functional team in pricing strategy development requires a unique set of leadership skills.

Here are some essential skills for effective pricing management:

1. Visionary Leadership

A successful leader must articulate a clear vision for the pricing strategy. This vision should align with the company's overall goals and market positioning. Communicating this vision effectively helps team members understand the importance of their work and how it contributes to the organization's success.

2. Emotional Intelligence

Emotional intelligence is crucial for understanding team dynamics and managing interpersonal relationships. A leader with high emotional intelligence can navigate conflicts, motivate team members, and foster a positive team culture. This skill is particularly important in a cross-functional team, where diverse perspectives may lead to disagreements.

3. Decision-Making Skills

Pricing decisions can significantly impact a company's profitability and market position. As a leader, you must make informed decisions based on data analysis, market insights, and team input. This requires a balance of analytical thinking and intuition, allowing you to weigh the pros and cons of various pricing strategies.

4. Adaptability

The business landscape is constantly changing, and pricing strategies must evolve accordingly. A good leader should be adaptable, willing to pivot when market conditions shift or when new information emerges. This flexibility enables the team to stay competitive and responsive to customer needs.

5. Empowering Team Members

Empowering team members to take ownership of their roles fosters a sense of responsibility and accountability. Encourage team members to share their insights and take the lead on specific projects or initiatives. This empowerment not only boosts morale but also enhances the overall effectiveness of the team.

Implementing the Pricing Strategy

Once the team has developed a pricing strategy, the next step is implementation. This phase requires careful planning and execution to ensure that the strategy is effectively communicated and adopted across the organization.

1. Developing a Communication Plan

A comprehensive communication plan is essential for ensuring that all stakeholders understand the new pricing strategy. This plan should include:

- Internal Communication: Keep all departments informed about the pricing changes, rationale, and expected outcomes. This transparency fosters buy-in and reduces resistance to change.

- Training Sessions: Conduct training sessions for sales and customer service teams to equip them with the knowledge and tools they need to communicate the new pricing effectively to customers.

- Customer Communication: Develop a strategy for communicating pricing changes to customers. This communication should emphasize the value of the product or service and address any potential concerns customers may have.

2. Monitoring and Evaluation

After implementation, it's crucial to monitor the performance of the pricing strategy and evaluate its effectiveness. This involves:

- Setting Key Performance Indicators (KPIs): Establish KPIs that align with the objectives of the pricing strategy. These may include sales volume, profit margins, customer acquisition rates, and customer satisfaction scores.

- Collecting Feedback: Regularly gather feedback from team members, customers, and other stakeholders to assess the impact of the pricing strategy. This feedback can provide valuable insights for future adjustments.

- Continuous Improvement: Pricing strategies should not be static. Use the data collected to refine and optimize the pricing approach continuously. This iterative process ensures that the strategy remains relevant and effective in a changing market.

Conclusion

Leading a cross-functional team in pricing strategy development is a complex but rewarding endeavor. By building a diverse team, fostering collaboration, and honing essential leadership skills, you can create a dynamic environment that drives successful pricing strategies. Remember that pricing is not just a number; it's a reflection of your brand's value proposition and a critical component of your overall business strategy.

As you embark on this journey, keep in mind that the landscape of pricing is ever-evolving. Stay informed about industry trends, consumer behavior, and competitive dynamics to ensure your pricing strategies remain effective and aligned with your organization's goals. With the right leadership and a collaborative team approach, you can master the art and science of pricing, ultimately achieving competitive success and market dominance.

Chapter 22: Future Trends in Pricing Strategies

As we navigate the complexities of an ever-evolving marketplace, understanding the future trends in pricing strategies is crucial for businesses seeking competitive advantage and sustainable profitability. The landscape of pricing is not static; it is influenced by technological advancements, changing consumer behaviors, and global economic shifts. In this chapter, we will explore the emerging trends in pricing models and strategies, and discuss how organizations can prepare for the future of pricing in a competitive market.

The Rise of Technology-Driven Pricing

In recent years, technology has dramatically transformed how businesses approach pricing. The introduction of artificial intelligence (AI) and machine learning (ML) has enabled companies to analyze vast amounts of data to optimize their pricing strategies in real-time. These technologies allow for more sophisticated pricing models that can adapt to market conditions, consumer behavior, and competitor actions.

1. Dynamic Pricing Powered by AI: Dynamic pricing strategies, which involve adjusting prices based on demand, competition, and other external factors, are becoming increasingly prevalent. AI algorithms can analyze historical sales data, current market trends, and even social media sentiment to determine the optimal price at any given moment. This level of responsiveness can significantly enhance profitability, particularly in industries such as travel, hospitality, and e-commerce.

2. Personalized Pricing: Another trend is the move towards personalized pricing, where companies tailor prices based on individual customer profiles, preferences, and purchasing behaviors. This approach leverages customer data to create unique pricing offers that resonate with specific segments of the market. While personalized pricing can enhance customer satisfaction and loyalty, it also raises ethical considerations regarding fairness and transparency.

3. Subscription Pricing Models: The subscription economy is on the rise, with businesses across various sectors adopting subscription-based pricing models. This approach provides customers with ongoing access to

products or services for a recurring fee, creating predictable revenue streams for companies. As consumers increasingly value convenience and flexibility, businesses must consider how subscription pricing can fit into their overall pricing strategy.

The Impact of Consumer Behavior

As consumer preferences evolve, so too must pricing strategies. Understanding the psychological and behavioral factors that influence purchasing decisions is essential for developing effective pricing models.

1. Value Perception: Consumers are becoming more discerning, often seeking greater value for their money. This shift necessitates a focus on value-based pricing strategies that emphasize the benefits and unique selling propositions of products or services. Companies must effectively communicate the value they provide to justify their pricing and foster customer loyalty.

2. Sustainability and Ethical Considerations: Today's consumers are increasingly concerned about sustainability and ethical practices. Businesses that prioritize environmentally friendly practices and social responsibility may find that they can command higher prices. Transparency in pricing, especially regarding sustainability efforts, can foster trust and enhance brand

reputation.

3. Experience-Driven Pricing: As experiences become a central aspect of consumer spending, businesses must consider how to price experiences rather than just products. This trend is particularly relevant in industries such as travel, entertainment, and dining, where the overall experience can significantly impact perceived value. Companies should explore how to enhance the customer experience and align pricing strategies accordingly.

Globalization and Market Expansion

The global marketplace presents both opportunities and challenges for pricing strategies. As businesses expand into new markets, they must navigate diverse economic conditions, cultural differences, and competitive landscapes.

1. Localized Pricing Strategies: Companies entering international markets must adopt localized pricing strategies that consider regional economic factors, consumer purchasing power, and cultural preferences. A one-size-fits-all approach to pricing may not be effective; instead, businesses should conduct thorough market research to understand local dynamics and tailor their pricing accordingly.

2. Currency Fluctuations: Global businesses must also account for currency fluctuations when setting prices. Exchange rate volatility can impact profit margins, necessitating strategies such as pricing in local currencies or implementing hedging techniques to mitigate risk.

3. Cross-Border Pricing Regulations: Companies must stay informed about pricing regulations in different countries, as these can vary significantly. Understanding local laws regarding pricing practices, such as price discrimination and minimum advertised pricing, is essential for compliance and avoiding legal pitfalls.

The Role of Data Analytics in Pricing

Data analytics will continue to play a pivotal role in shaping pricing strategies. The ability to collect, analyze, and interpret data provides businesses with valuable insights into market trends, consumer behavior, and competitive dynamics.

1. Predictive Analytics: Predictive analytics allows businesses to forecast future pricing trends based on historical data and market indicators. By leveraging predictive models, companies can make informed pricing decisions that align with anticipated changes in demand and competition.

2. Real-Time Pricing Insights: The integration of real-time

data analytics enables businesses to monitor pricing performance continuously. This capability allows for agile pricing adjustments in response to market fluctuations, ensuring that companies remain competitive and maximize profitability.

3. Customer Segmentation: Advanced data analytics can facilitate more effective customer segmentation, enabling businesses to identify distinct consumer groups and tailor pricing strategies accordingly. By understanding the unique needs and preferences of different segments, companies can optimize pricing to enhance customer satisfaction and drive sales.

Preparing for the Future of Pricing

To thrive in the future of pricing, businesses must adopt a proactive approach that embraces innovation, flexibility, and customer-centricity. Here are key strategies for preparing for the evolving pricing landscape:

1. Invest in Technology: Companies should invest in advanced pricing technologies, including AI and data analytics tools, to enhance their pricing capabilities. By leveraging technology, businesses can gain a competitive edge and respond more effectively to market changes.

2. Foster a Culture of Agility: Organizations must cultivate

a culture of agility that encourages experimentation and adaptability. Pricing strategies should be viewed as dynamic and subject to continuous improvement based on market feedback and performance analysis.

3. Enhance Cross-Functional Collaboration: Effective pricing requires collaboration across various departments, including marketing, sales, finance, and product development. Building cross-functional teams that can share insights and work together on pricing strategies will lead to more informed decision-making and better outcomes.

4. Focus on Customer Engagement: Engaging with customers to understand their needs, preferences, and perceptions of value is critical for effective pricing. Companies should prioritize customer feedback and incorporate it into their pricing strategies to ensure alignment with market expectations.

5. Monitor Industry Trends: Staying informed about industry trends and emerging pricing models is essential for maintaining competitiveness. Businesses should regularly assess market dynamics and be prepared to adapt their pricing strategies to align with changing consumer behaviors and industry developments.

Conclusion

The future of pricing strategies is poised for transformation as businesses navigate a landscape shaped by technology, consumer behavior, and globalization. By embracing innovative pricing models, leveraging data analytics, and prioritizing customer engagement, organizations can position themselves for success in an increasingly competitive market. As we move forward, the ability to adapt and respond to emerging trends will be key to mastering pricing strategies and achieving market dominance. The journey of pricing is ongoing, and those who invest in understanding and optimizing their pricing strategies will emerge as leaders in their respective industries.

www.ingramcontent.com/pod-product-compliance
Lightning Source LLC
Chambersburg PA
CBHW071022240526
45469CB00006BD/2048